INTERNATIONAL BANKING AND RURAL DEVELOPMENT

The Making of Modern Africa

Series Editors: Abebe Zegeye and John Higginson

International Banking and Rural Development
The World Bank in Sub-Saharan Africa

PADE BADRU
University of Louisville

Routledge
Taylor & Francis Group

LONDON AND NEW YORK

First published 1998 by Ashgate Publishing

Reissued 2018 by Routledge
2 Park Square, Milton Park, Abingdon, Oxon, OX14 4RN
711 Third Avenue, New York, NY 10017, USA

Routledge is an imprint of the Taylor & Francis Group, an informa business

Publisher's Note
The publisher has gone to great lengths to ensure the quality of this reprint but points out that some imperfections in the original copies may be apparent.

Disclaimer
The publisher has made every effort to trace copyright holders and welcomes correspondence from those they have been unable to contact.

A Library of Congress record exists under LC control number: 97076937

ISBN 13: 978-1-138-31431-3 (hbk)
ISBN 13: 978-0-429-45703-6 (ebk)

Contents

Chapter 3

Chapter 4

Chapter 8

List of Tables

Acknowledgement

I would like to thank, first of all, all the faculty and staff members of the department of sociology at the State University of New York at Stony Brook, without whose cooperation and friendliness during my four years in the department, this work would not have been possible. I would also like to extend my gratitude and appreciation to all the members of my dissertation committee, whose constant criticisms gave me all the courage and inspiration needed to produce this work. My special thanks go to my advisor, an outstanding sociologist and African scholar, Dr. Bruce Hare, whose constant words of encouragement saw me through the most difficult time while writing this dissertation. My thanks also go to Drs. Richard Williams, Mary Vogel, Paget Henry and Ian Roxborough, all of whom, in their different styles and ways, contributed enormously to improving the quality of this work. I would also like to express my thanks to my colleagues in the department of Pan African Studies, University of Louisville, Louisville, Kentucky, for their support of my work. I am also grateful to the office of the Dean of Arts and Sciences, University of Louisville, for making available to me a mini-grant towards the preparation of this book. Finally, I would like to thank Ms. Wanda Olivera, the secretary to the Graduate programme in sociology at the State Uinversity of New York - Stony Brook for the time she took in typing the original manuscript.

Of course, I alone am responsible for all the empirical and conceptual faults and errors contained in this book.

List of Abbreviations

ADP	Agricultural Development Project
EEC	European Economic Commission
ECLA	Economic Commission for Africa
FFB	Fresh Food Bunches
GR	Green Revolution
IITA	Institute for Tropical Agriculture
IMF	International Monetary Fund
IRBD	International Bank for Reconstructing and Development
IRDP	Integrated Rural Development
NAFAPP	National Food Acceleration Programme
Naira	Nigerian Currency
OFN	Operation Feed the Nation
RISADEP	Rivers State Rural Development Project
RISONPALM	Rivers State Palm Oil Development Corporation
SAP	Structural Adjustment Programme
SPO	Special Palm Oil
UNDP	United Nations Development Programme
UNO	United nations
U.S.$	United States of America's dollar
WB	World Bank

1 Introduction: The World Bank and the Third World

The World Bank involvement in Third World development can be traced back to the early fifties when the bank officially became an instrument of global capitalist development. The establishment of the bank, and its sister institution, the International Monetary Fund (IMF), represented a crucial realignment of forces within the world capitalist economy at the time with the United States replacing the global hegemony of the British imperial state. The rise of the United States as a major economic, political, and military power after the war, thus set the stage for the ideological battle against the spread of communism worldwide. The cold war, as this era was popularly known, pitched the capitalist west against Soviet and eastern block communism with the Third World caught in the middle of ideological battles between the two superpowers.

In order to reduce the attraction of communism as an option of social, political, economic development for poor countries in the developing world, and war ravaged Europe and Japan, the establishment of a capitalist institution that would promote capitalist development worldwide became the preoccupation of the United States and its European allies. The spread of Soviet communism into eastern Europe, and the sudden rise of the Soviet Union as a major superpower after the end of the war, clearly posed a big threat to traditional European interests in the former colonies and dependencies. Thus, by promoting a vigorous capitalist transformation of agriculture in the developing world in addition to some limited capitalist development in industry and commerce, the western powers believed it would be able to discourage the new states in Africa, and elsewhere in Asia, and Latin American from joining the communist block. It is against this background that we situate our analysis of the World Bank's changing strategies in the development process of many Third World countries.

1

The Origin of the World Bank

The International Bank for Reconstruction and Development (IRDB), otherwise known as the World Bank, is by no doubt the single most powerful instrument of global capitalist development. It is indeed the largest single source of development resources in a world divided by extremes of riches and poverty. As a pillar of global capitalist world domination, the bank continues to play the role of an intermediary between the developed western metropolis section of the global economy and its poorest parts in the peripheries of Africa, Latin America and of southeast Asia. Playing the role of an intermediary evidently demands that the bank maintains the existing relations of production, technology control, investment, exchange, and the economic advantage of the developed world globally.

The World Bank came into being out of the Bretton Woods agreement of 1944, shortly before the end of World War II. Indeed, right from its inception, the bank reflected, and continues to reflect, the economic hegemony of the United States of America whose economic vision of the world order runs counter to those of the majority of nations in the developing world. As the only nation who came out of the war relatively unbruised, the U.S. used its economic and military might to determine the contents and forms of the bank's operating policies which clearly put her in a position to define development agenda globally.

Originally, the bank was established to oversee and regulate lending to war ruined Europe. Its primary function then was to reduce the risks of financial crisis that might embroil the global capitalist system since Europe was just emerging from a tremendous economic ruin brought about by the war. In addition to this function, the bank was also empowered to establish lending standards that private commercial banks and national central banks will follow in addition to communicating investment opportunities worldwide. While the two cardinal objectives of the bank are "reconstruction" and "development", it soon became clear that its initial focus and emphasis was on reconstruction and not development. Up until the mid-sixties, the emphasis of IBRD was on building Europe, while Third World development was nothing but a secondary goal of the bank.

Once the bank's attention turned to Third World development, it became clear that a different set of criteria was adopted in terms of its lending policy toward the least developed nations. As it turned out, more stringent conditions were often attached to lending for development projects contrary to what the practice was during the reconstruction of Europe after the war. Indeed, lending to the least developed nations are usually tied up to the adoption of specific development models that emphasize free market principles even though this model, in many cases, is completely out of order with the true conditions and realities in these countries. The assumption behind this approach is that what worked well in Europe should also work for nations in the developing world. This is exactly where the problem lay. It soon became clear that the bank's generosity in rebuilding Europe was replaced with harsher guidelines, unbelievably high interest on money borrowed from the bank once it comes to Third World development.

The Bank's Changing Strategies

In the main, the bank's belated focus on Third World development was rather a welcome gesture on the part of Third World leaders who saw brighter prospects arising from the bank's activities. However, the bank's development strategies, and policy guidelines toward the least developed nations have shifted over the years, calling to question the bank's sincerity. In the early post war era, 1950-1965, the bank emphasized large scale investment especially in infrastructure, namely highways development, port expansion, upgrading of airport facilities, railways, and tele-communication. The underlying principle behind this policy focus was that with the modernization of infrastructure, the volume of commerce would create the conditions for a capitalist development. During this phase, the bulk of the bank's lending to the least developed world went into specific projects approved by the bank's board, especially projects defined as development driven. The majority of these projects were often contracted to the bank's approved foreign developers who were well known for charging exorbitant fees. In most cases, foreign currency borrowed for these projects were often recycled back to the metropolitan economies in the form of experts' fees and debt repayments..

In fact, the bulk of the debts incurred by many developing nations today were incurred during this phase. Market principles imposed by the bank as preconditions for lending money to these poor nations were largely responsible for the distortions and development gaps between the urban and rural sectors of many Third World economies. This rigid laissez-faire economic models forced by the banks on these nations were obviously inappropriate in terms of resolving internal economic contradictions. In the end, the bank's policies so far have not been able

3

to set the stage for a viable and sustainable development.

In spite of the optimism surrounding free market based development in the developing world, by the seventies the crises of transformation in these formations actually intensified to the dismay of the bank's officials who had blindly hoped for an economic miracle. Indeed, during the implementation of this phase, national agricultural production declined in the periphery, as we shall show in the particular case of Nigeria which is the focus of this book. Market based development paradigms, adopted by many developing nations in the sixties and seventies, only complicated their development efforts. It was the realization of growing inequality, and widespread poverty in the seventies that led the bank to change its development approach in the Third World. Under the leadership of its new president, Robert McNamara, former U.S. defense secretary under the Kennedy administration, the bank redefined its approach to Third World development.

The failure of the bank's policy in generating growth and development in the least developed world led to a change in its basic development policy. A new policy dubbed "distribution with growth", and "basic human needs" championed by McNamara, was adopted. The new approach emphasized selective lending for agricultural development projects, which according to McNamara, was geared towards alleviating the plight of the bottom 40 percent of the world's poorest. In fact, by the early seventies, nearly one billion people in the developing world were believed to be living in abject poverty, and in conditions of squalor unimaginable before (Don Babai, 1993). In pursuit of this new policy, the Integrated Rural Development Programme (IRDP) was adopted as a guiding principle for agricultural transformation in the developing world.

Even though the IRDP targeted rural production, the programme also focused on several issues such as health, portable water, sanitation, population control, and nutrition. The new programme aimed at promoting small scale capitalist farming enterprises in the rural areas. These farms, the bank officials hoped, would take advantage of improved new seedlings, intermediate technology, and the use of fertilizers. Indeed, the belief was that by creating a small stratum of highly efficient capitalist farmers, rural poverty would be reduced. The bank was utterly wrong. The irony of the programme lay in the fact that lending to peasant farmers was based on market principles of adequate return on investment. As it turned out, the bulk of loans dispensed during this phase went only to rich peasant farmers, and urban based absentee landlords whom the bank believed had the capability of paying back the loans.

4

This strategy backfired since poor and middle strata peasants who lacked the collateral for farming loans were left out of the project. This lending practice coupled with the bank's emphasis on export related activities contradict the main objectives of the programme which among other things, was the reduction of rural poverty. As will be shown in the data presented here, rather than alleviating the conditions of the rural poor, the IRDP actually contributed to the widening of inequality and poverty.

By the 1980s, several developing economies were at the verge of collapse as a result of debt repayment on loans accrued from rural development. Sensing a serious crisis in the periphery, the World Bank introduced a new programme that focused on re-articulating peripheral economies back into the world system. The new programme, dubbed "Structural Adjustment Programme", was intended to save these economies from total collapse. The Structural Adjustment Programme (SAP) initially aimed at steering debt ridden Third World economies back on the road to capitalist development based on laissez faire principles. The main focus of SAP is the elimination of waste in the public sector, and the reduction of the role of government in the development process.

It should be emphasized that this phase of adjustment was occasioned by structural crisis within the global capitalist system, more importantly, the necessity to resolve certain contradictions that were increasingly embroiling the global capitalist system from the periphery. It is hardly a coincidence that the peak of the implementation of SAP was also the time the "new world order" principles were being implemented in the metropolis of the world economy. More than a decade after its implementation, SAP has not been able to achieve its main objective, which is to improve economic conditions among other things. However the bank would like us to believe otherwise. In fact, this phase of adjustment has led to a widening of the gap between the developed and the least developed nations most of whom have experienced adjustment induced inflation as a result of the diminishing value of their national currencies. Internally, SAP has clearly widened the income gap between the poor and the rich, and between the rural and urban sectors of the economy in countries that have implemented the programme. Clearly, there is a definite relationship between political turmoil in the periphery of the world economy and the implementation of SAP. This thus begs the question of whether development can be achieved under the conditions created by the bank's policies.

The World Bank and Africa

Since the sixties, the bank's African development focus has, in many cases, produced negative consequences. For instance in the two areas where the bank had taken the lead namely, hydro-dam projects and ADPs, the results have been less than promising. Instead of promoting development, the bank's paternalistic approach to African development, particularly rural transformation, has destroyed many African economies by encouraging export related activities. Several cases of poorly informed policy recommendations to African governments contributed to the intensity of the crisis which many of them face today. A few examples will do to demonstrate this.

In Ethiopia during the sixties, the World Bank encouraged the conversion of the Awash River Valley into a huge sugar cane, cotton and banana plantation. The project called for the construction of several dams that would provide electricity to the capital city of Addis Ababa, and irrigation to the plantations in the swampy central Ethiopia region. Before the dams were constructed, the Awash River Valley supported nearly 150,000 farmers and pastoralists. With the construction of the dams, several of these pastorals were given notice to vacate their traditional homeland with the promise of resettlement elsewhere. At least 25,000 of the pastoralists were removed from their homes, and left with no other means of supporting their traditional ways of life (Adams, 1992:97). By the late 1980s, the adjoining areas to the Awash River Valley were already over-grazed because of the roaming band of the pastorals who had earlier on been displaced from the villages to give way to the dams. The Ethiopian famine of the eighties was the by-product of the displacement of these pastorals.

Despite the fact that the Awash River Valley hydro-dam project did not produce the desired result, the World Bank went ahead and implemented the same project in other parts of sub-Saharan Africa. In northern Nigeria for instance, the bank assisted in the construction of two controversial dams, the Kainji and Bakolori dams. The construction of the Kainji dam led to the displacement of 42,000 farmers and pastoralists who were forcibly removed from their homes (Adams, ibid.). The Bakolori dam was even more controversial than the Kainji dam. When the Bakolori villagers refused to be relocated, the state government sent in para-military police who attacked the villagers, killing hundreds of them. A few months after the dam was completed, it collapsed as a result of poor engineering work, overflooding the areas where the farmers had been relocated killing many more of them (Beckman, 1985:76-104). The farmers were never

6

compensated for loss of their properties or relatives who died during the flooding.

The construction of similar dams in southern and central Africa also led to massive displacement. The construction of the Kariba dam in Zimbabwe in the fifties resulted in the displacement of 56,000 peasant farmers. Those who resisted the relocation orders were massacred by state police. In Ghana, the construction of the Akosombo dam resulted in 80,000 farmers losing their homes and livelihood. In Zaire, 13,000 farmers were displaced during the construction of the Ruizzi Dam II (Adams, ibid.). The environmental costs of these hydro-dam projects have hardly been investigated, but what is clear is that these dams have not produced the benefits the World Bank envisaged that they would. For example, in the case of the Akosombo dam in Ghana, environmentalists have linked the receding coastline stretching from Ghana, Togo and Nigeria to the construction of the Akosombo dam.

Perhaps the most flagrant disrespect for state autonomy by the World Bank was in the case of Sudan, whose economy is in total ruin today after two decades of implementing the bank's ill-advised hydro projects. The Sudanese government was encouraged by the bank to switch to cotton production as a means of resolving the economic crisis of the early seventies. Loans made available under the programme by the bank, as Adams (1992) pointed out, only went to rich farmers and merchants who had the financial capacity, and land to mechanize production. Those poor farmers whose lands were too small to take advantage of the loans saw their land either taken over by the rich farmers or simply confiscated by the state. The immediate effect of the Sudanese experience was widespread food shortages in the eighties which led finally to the civil unrest, and consequently, the on-going war in the south. In fact, with the implementation of the programme, the Sudanese current account deficit in 1983 rose to 11 percent of the GNP from just six percent before the project was introduced. In addition to this, the rate of inflation also rose while the national currency underwent three successive devaluations.

While the bank continues to distance itself from the failures of these projects, it is clear that its over-reliance on unprovable macroeconomic principles may defeat the purpose of its policies in Africa. Patricia Adams notes:

> Despite the best intentions, the World Bank was set up to exercise
> financial power without liability and political power without
> responsibilities. Its loans - free from public sector scrutinity and
> private sector discipline - and its triple-A credit rating - the result of

7

political commitments rather than prudent investments - have allowed the bank to finance money-losing enterprises that can only be defended by invoking exaggerated macroeconomic claims. The bank's unaccountability to the citizens of its member states, a consequence of its legal and financial structure, has undermined the development of democratic institutions, healthy economies and well managed environment throughout sub-Saharan Africa. (Adams, 1992: 98).

This has been the tragic experience of African neo-colonial states with the World Bank, the so-called agent of development. In this final section we will discuss the case study of this book which is Nigeria.

Nigeria: The Case Study

In the late seventies, the crude petroleum fuelled development programme of the Nigerian state was beginning to show some signs of cracking. When the bottom finally fell off, state officials turned to the World Bank for assistance. As in many African neo-colonial states, the crisis of economy, polity and society sharpened so rapidly that the neo-colonial state was left with no alternative but to result to violence, and arbitrary rule under the dictatorship of the military. The "Asian miracle" that many development experts believed would soon sweep through Africa never occurred. Instead, the all pervasive crisis of polity and society continues to complicate the process of economic transformation even in countries with sufficient human and natural resources to pursue a post-colonial capitalist development.

In Nigeria, the past decade or so has witnessed worsening economic conditions resulting in steady decline of the civil society and state. This decline followed relatively prosperous years of crude petroleum sponsored development of the 1970s. Indeed, the relatively good life of the seventies has now been replaced with debt servicing which currently represents nearly 40 percent of Gross National Product. The dream of a crude oil financed capitalist development of that era has now turned into a struggle for national survival. The most visible indicator of this crisis is the rapidly declining agrarian sector of the national economy.

The reality today is that agricultural production is declining at an alarming rate while population growth continues at a pace that could not be supported by growth in food production. The overall argument of this book is that this agrarian decline in Nigeria is due partly to a fundamental dislocation of the structure of the economy; a dislocation brought about by the sudden found wealth in crude oil in the early seventies. It also argues that structural constraints, imposed by the peculiar position of the Nigerian dependent economy within the world system, also played a significant role in precipitating the current agrarian crisis. It is a well established fact that before and during colonial epochs, Nigeria was well sufficient in food production. However, by the early seventies, it had lost her capacity to feed the population, while growth continued in the crude petroleum sector. The expectations that political independence from the viciousness of colonial rule will bring economic progress remain unfulfilled. While the country gained political independence from Britain in 1960, and became a republic in October of 1963, the colonial relations of dependence actually increased to the dismay of the nationalist elite who fought for independence. As it turned out, political independence from European colonization did not bring about the desired economic freedom.

In post-independence Nigeria, the dream of economic transformation was based on promoting rapid industrialization using earned revenue from crude petroleum. The policy choice of the post-colonial state is one that continues to emphasize urban based model of economic development at the expense of the rural sector of the economy. The realization of the failure of this approach, in the eighties, led policy makers to refocus their development efforts on rural transformation. This shift in development strategy of the state also meant a reliance on international institutions and transnational corporations for the provision of modern technology and know-how. The World Bank and International Monetary Fund (IMF), in particular, have been the vanguards of this new form of economic cooperation. The assistance provided by the World Bank came in the form of Agricultural Development Projects (ADPs) aimed at generating the capacity for rural reproduction.

Increasingly, the ADPs have come under severe criticisms from scholars who maintain that rather than assisting in the process of economic transformation, these projects are actually creating obstacles in the path of national development. The critics claim that ADPs, and the current World Bank's fiscal policy of Structural Adjustment Programme (SAP), have contributed to the deepening of economic crisis in many Third World countries. The critics of World Bank's agricultural projects have pointed to the inappropriateness of recommended techniques, farm inputs choice and extension advice offered to peasants, which they argue, are only suitable for export crops production. On the other hand, officials responsible for the execution and design of these ADPs contend that the adoption of this model is a sure road to resolving the crisis of agrarian transformation. This present work, therefore, investigates these competing claims by evaluating two World Bank's funded agricultural development projects in southeastern Nigeria, where agrarian decline is reaching an alarming state.

It is the contention of this book that this new form of post colonial cooperation with international finance institutions is generating new forms of dependence and loss of state autonomy, since externally defined development projects hardly address the immediate needs of the recipient countries. The reality is that some of the economic policies forced on the state by foreign experts contained elements that may undermine the stability of the state. These "development diplomats", as the bank likes to refer to them, often relied on economic indices and categories that were extrapolated from other peoples' experience in dealing with the African situation. The overall result of this approach is a complication of the development process. In many instances, as we show above, the recommended approach has led to the reinforcement of existing social and economic inequalities in many poor nations that have turned to the bank for assistance.

In addition to this, the bank's policy recommendations have the potential of increasing the economic burden on the poor, and thereby, creating the conditions for political agitation. This may explain why many Third World governments are prone to acquiring a "get tough" attitude in dealing with popular resentments that may develop from the imposition of this new economic model. Indeed, for some developing countries, the role of international banking, in the context of national development has been worrisome to say the least. As Pratt notes:

> The Bank has become increasingly arrogant and ideological in its approach to development issues in the Third World. Increasingly, the Bank operates on the assumption that it already knows the policies it wishes to insist upon before it enters negotiations with individual Third World countries....When an IMF mission comes to a country to negotiate a standby credit, its negotiators actually arrive with a prepared text for the letter they wish the finance minister of that country to send to the IMF.... Bank officials have no doubt about the policy changes they wish to require of a country... Bank officials not only suffer from a messianic complex but also every few years they change their gods. The present god they worship is export promotion (Pratt, 1983:56).

The contradiction between state autonomy and the adoption of externally imposed development options often have the potential of creating serious dilemma for relations between the state and internal social classes. What is seen as good and sound economic policy by the bank officials often failed to address local conditions, and indigenous poverty, as former Jamaican Prime Minister, Michael Manley, expressed his frustration with the bank thus:

> IMF prescriptions are designed by and for developed economies and are inappropriate for developing countries of any kind; the severe suffering imposed on a developing society through IMF conditionality is endured without any real prospect of a favourable economic outcome and without adequate foundation for social-welfare provisions to mitigate the hardships experienced by the people (Manley, 1980:5).

In order to verify the contending views of the bank's project, this author undertook a longitudinal study of two carefully selected World Bank's agricultural development projects that are typical of the Bank's approach to rural development. The study examines the socio-economic impact of the projects on two peasants' communities in southeast Nigeria. Based on the analysis the data collected in the course of this research, the author intends to examine the extent to which these projects have contributed to the process of economic development or underdevelopment in the project area. This author understands development as encompassing several aspects of social life including but not limited to economic independence, state autonomy, mass political participation, sustainable economic transformation and improved living standards in a free and mutually dependent world.

Research Objectives

The first objective of this research is to examine the extent to which the ADPs have achieved their stated objectives, by looking at the socio-economic impact of the programme on the project villages. The second objective is to determine how the implementation of the Structural Adjustment Programme has impacted on the agricultural development projects particularly the effect of currency devaluation on farmers' income, commodity prices and the relations between the urban and rural sectors of the economy. This research falls under two broad categories namely; economic sociology and social change.

For the field study, two ADPs were selected as case studies. In preparation for the fieldwork, this researcher looked at existing studies of rural households in Nigeria. These studies provided us with an idea of the general income distribution and average peasant incomes prior to the introduction of the ADPs. The knowledge of the pre-project income distribution was necessary for the evaluation of the economic impact of the project on participating peasant's households. In addition, World Bank documents dealing with the planning and execution of the projects were intensively studied. These documents are published periodically by the World Bank, and they are available at the extension offices where the projects are located.

In addition to these, most of the appraisal studies commissioned by the World Bank, and those commissioned independently by the Nigerian Ministry of Agriculture and Natural Resources were also reviewed. However, a good part of the fieldwork in Nigeria focused on the Port Harcourt offices of the Rivers State Agricultural Development Projects (RISADEP), most especially, its "General Extension" and the "Farm Management Services" divisions. The two offices directly oversee various operations on the sites, as well as ensure peasant participation in the project.

The survey of peasant households reported in this research used open-ended interviews. The aim of the survey is to ascertain how various strata of the peasantry had been affected by the projects. In order to evaluate the success or failure of the projects, attention was focused on the economic benefits which the projects had brought to participating peasants. From the data collected the author was able to assess the overall change in the quality of life as measured by income distribution within the project sites (gross community produce), peasants' household incomes, quality of health provision, education, water resources, availability of farm equipment, and new technology and accessibility to farm extension services. All of these measures were compared to those of peasants in the control village, an agricultural community that has yet to implement a similar programme.

Research Design and a Description of the Project Area

I have selected two projects in this area for an intensive study. Both projects are very typical of the bank's ADPs, and therefore conclusions drawn from these two could be extended to the others in the area. All the ADPs in the country follow exactly the same design format and organization structure. The two projects selected are the nucleus oil palm development project located at Ubima, and the smallholding oil palm estates at Elele, both in Rivers State, south east Nigeria. During the colonial era, the region was known for its oil palm, and palm kernel production. However, with the civil war which lasted from 1967 to 1970, and with the discovery of crude petroleum in the area, oil palm production diminished considerably. Because the livelihood of the majority of the peasant farmers in this area depended largely on oil palm production, post-war rehabilitation of oil palm estates became the concern of both the state and federal governments. In 1974, the Federal government formally requested the assistance of the World Bank for the rehabilitation of oil palm production in the area. Although the request came in the form of a general agricultural revitalization programme of the federal government, nevertheless the emphasis was on the production of export crops.

The Rivers State Oil Development Project (the nucleus estate), and the Elele Smallholder Oil Palm Estates are both located in the southern savannah area where climatic conditions are conducive to arable farming. Both projects are funded by the World Bank. The Rivers State Agricultural Development Programme (RISEDEP) is currently supervising the Smallholding Estates at Elele. For both projects, technical advice is supplied by World Bank, which also supervises locally trained personnel. The fieldwork is aimed at discovering what differences exist between the two project villages and the control village in addition to understanding the degree of social and economic transformation that has taken place in the two project villages since the programme began. In documenting these differences, this research also used indicators such as the level of health care provision, the overall production pattern, numbers of wage labourers being hired, revenue and profit accruing to the projects, and the amount of this profit that is made available to each peasant household participating in the project. Item checks were found to be more useful than closed-ended questionnaires in generating certain information such as fertility rate. Others items checked include the size of peasants' families, authority pattern within the household, number of adults engaged in production, and the degree of women's participation in the project.

Significance of this Research

This study hopes to provide findings that may be useful to policy planners in Nigeria, and possibly, in other developing countries. It also hopes to contribute to a better understanding of the process of peasant transformation, and the role of multinational corporations in rural transformation in these societies. Given the paucity of sociological theory on Third World development, especially those dealing with Africa, this author thinks that it is time to move beyond traditional theories that often ignore the reality of Third World formations. I believe it is time we had a much broader sociological understanding of the economic problems confronting these formations; an understanding that is necessary, if we are to comprehend the complexity and pertinence of rural transformation in these formations. Without this understanding, the World Bank's goal of promoting sustainable growth in the developing world, no matter how well intentioned, will be as elusive as ever. In this regard, this study is more compelling and appropriate in the light of the deteriorating conditions in this part of the world.

Having said this, this author believes that no sociological work is worthwhile, if it fails to provide concrete proposals to address the problematic specified in its main hypothesis. In this regard, this research hopes to contribute to the development of a new paradigm through which sustainable growth and development can be achieved for the people in the developing world.

Problems with Data Collection

From January to mid April of 1991, this author visited the project sites in south eastern Nigeria to collect data for this research. Prior to this, one site was visited during an earlier study in 1984. Two research assistants were hired for this fieldwork, both of whom came from the community of our studies. Even though I could speak the indigenous language, nevertheless, being a foreigner was apparently a barrier. For instance during a village meeting at Ubima I was asked to leave because the tradition forbids "strangers" listening in while the elders conduct the village affairs. This led to my decision to recruit assistants who were much more familiar with the customs and tradition of the villagers or what the villagers called "sons of the soil". These assistants were able to sit in for me in situations when I was considered an unwanted participant.

There are always difficulties associated with studying peasant villages in Africa. Some of these difficulties often arose from the complete distrust of city residents, whom the villagers take to be tax collectors for the government. This mistrust has its root in colonial days when British colonialists used educated city residents to chase down villagers who avoided paying hut taxes. Villagers are not very comfortable when it comes to discussing their income. Neither are they

14

comfortable discussing personal questions such as the numbers of wives or children they have.

Gaining the trust of the villagers is the most difficult aspect of doing fieldwork in Africa where there is age long tradition of distrust towards externally constituted authority, and an entrenched open hostility to government. There are two ways of breaking through this barrier. First, one may use a proxy method of relying entirely on locally recruited field assistants. The second option would be to take up residency in the community for a long period of time until one is able to form enough rapport with the community to the extent they give one their trust. The first option may require getting documentation and clearance from the local government. However, this may take some time because of the elaborate and inaccessible bureaucracy. The second option may be a little bit expensive, given the time limitation on research of this sort. The financial burden of having to take residency in a place one is not familiar with could prove to be insurmountable.

This researcher had two things on his side. First, having taught in the community for several years as a university lecturer, making contact was not as difficult. Second, the fact that two of my research assistants were my former students, and with their extensive connection in the project villages, some of the initial problems were ready overcome. The only problem I encountered was with project officials who were not particularly sure of what the researcher's goal or aim was all about. But after a few weeks of negotiations, they were finally convinced that the research was scholarly oriented.

Methodology

For each of the villages, the research team randomly selected thirty households for intensive study that lasted for several months. Besides, the researcher also interviewed project officials, local politicians, law enforcement officers and other people who were well connected or informed about the establishment of the projects in the area. We used survey method and participant observation. The participant observation involved attending village ceremonies, clan meetings, visiting peasant farms during work periods, attending numerous negotiation sessions between the extension workers and the villagers. In addition, the research team also sat on several of the weekly meetings of the peasants' cooperatives which have been set up by the projects' administrators. We also followed members of the households in their daily routines.

The interviews used an open-ended questionnaire. The respondents were given freedom to say whatever they wanted on the tape recorder. In cases where the respondents objected to taping the interview, the research team relied on detailed note taking. Each of the household's interviews lasted for about three hours, and in some cases, when the research team felt the need for a follow up on issues raised during the interviews, we routinely went back to pursue these.

In most of our selected cases, we tried as much as possible to corroborate what we were told from carefully selected informants. The duration of the interviews with the project's officials and local politicians varied from time to time depending on how long these individuals were willing to talk to us. Where these officials were unwilling to talk to us, they usually gave us documents which they thought could answer most of the questions we posed in our open-ended questionnaire. Six weeks into the fieldwork, enough rapport had been formed with the villagers to the extent that this researcher and his team were trusted enough to be invited to village functions such as burial, naming ceremonies, and the weekly village rituals from which we were previously excluded. We found that at these occasions, we were able to unobtrusively participate in the village life, and then use the observation to corroborate what someone may have told us the previous week. At the end of our field work, which involved several months of uninterrupted visits to the project villages and the offices of the project administrator, this researcher felt sufficiently confident as to the reliability of both the qualitative and quantitative data presented in the following chapters.

Plan of Work

This work is organized into eight chapters including the introduction. Chapter two presents the problem and procedure of data collection for this research. Chapter three examines the colonial and the post-colonial agricultural development policies of the Nigerian state, the aim of which is to show how these policies have contributed to the present crisis of transformation. In chapters four, five and six, three case studies of World Bank funded agricultural development projects (ADPs) are presented. Chapter seven discusses the findings, while chapter eight is the concluding chapter.

16

2 Controversies Regarding Rural Transformation and Capitalism in the Periphery of the World Economy

Overview

The latter part of the 20th century turned out to be the most difficult era for many African states since slavery and colonization. The continent as a whole witnessed several human disasters which obviously could have been prevented had attention been paid to the crisis of economy and society embedded in de-colonization. The economic crisis that continues to plague post independent African states has led to a review of traditional development theories. In the main, the African crisis continues to be understood from many theoretical perspectives. The dominant traditional mode of thought of the fifties and sixties, the modernization school, whose economic philosophy is tightly rooted in western positivism and neo-classical doctrine of the free market, is still the favourite of development experts. For this school, economic backwardness in the developing world is usually blamed on several factors such as a lack of technology, traditional cultural patterns, and uncontrolled population. Thus, for the modernization school, economic development is seen as a process of rapid urbanization through increased investment in the leading sectors of the national economy, most preferably the urban sector (Rostow, 1954). In short, modernization is expected to be accompanied by a rapid decline of the rural economy through increased communication (Lerner, 1963), and the breakdown of traditional authority structure and attitudes which are seen as impediments to economic development (Eisenstadt, 1964).

In contradistinction to the modernization mode of thought, radical scholars challenged the thesis of traditionalism which according to them ignores the historical patterns of global capitalist development. The dependency and

17

world system schools argue that economic transformation in the Third World is intricately linked to the global process of capitalist development (Frank, 1968; Wallerstein, 1974). The dependency scholars blamed underdevelopment in the periphery of the world economy on the historical conditions of colonialism, and more recently, on the operations of foreign multinational corporations in the developing world. The dominance of transnational corporations, and their monopolization of development resources globally, the school contends, was largely responsible for the creation of poverty and economic environment that made underdevelopment in the periphery inevitable. In the dependency and world system schema, capitalist development in its global dimension produces underdevelopment in the Third World. The dependency and the world system perspectives share the view that capitalist transformation of the rural economy is pertinent to the whole question of development. The possibility of rural transformation, in the periphery of the world economy, is being constrained by the obstacles imposed on these economies by the encroaching global capitalist mode of production. Development can be achieved, they argue, only if the link of dependence between the advanced world and the developing world is broken.

But breaking the link of colonial dependence is very problematic given the entrenchment of the Third World economies in the capitalist world system. The notion of a "break" is very crucial to the dependency theory, yet it does not really address the issue of what is to be done in the short run. Neither does such notion dispel or question the ability of capitalism to transform Third World agriculture, given the fact that both the economies of the advanced and developing world are intricately linked. Indeed, such a break from the historical link of dependence would require a revolution. The problem with this proposition is the fact that the dependency scholars failed to examine the difficulties involved in promoting a radical revolution in the periphery that would cut the link of dependence from the advanced economies of the West. Such prognosis by the dependency scholars is not only utopia, but dangerous since it ignores the alignment of social forces, and class relations, both nationally and internationally.

While the debates persist, economic conditions in many African states worsened considerably particularly in the past few decades. Thus the intensification of the agrarian crisis in the Third World, and the persistent shortfalls in food production, most recently in Africa, and elsewhere in the Third World, have led Africanist scholars to call into question the relevance of these economic and sociological theories of development (Amin, 1976; Onimade, 1984, 1988). This rapid deterioration in agrarian production in the Third World led to

18

intervention by the advanced Western nations, through various institutions such as the World Bank, International Monetary Fund (IMF), and the United Nations' Food and Agricultural Organization (FAO). These organizations provide short term bilateral aid, and assistance to the developing world on a scale that was never imagined before. But the emphasis of these external interventions in the developing world have focused primarily on the capitalization of agricultural production.

These international finance institutions, most especially the World Bank, and Western based multinational corporations, claim to be working towards building a viable economic basis for agrarian transformation in the developing world. Through its Integrated Rural Development Programme (IRDP), the World Bank agricultural policies continue to play a very dominant role in this process. But the strategy of promoting capitalist agriculture in the developing world had generated some debates and concerns amongst Africanist scholars. In particular, many Third World scholars have questioned the role of multinational corporations in the process of economic transformation; a role that they see as only reinforcing the historical condition of dependence (Onimade, 1988; Seidman, 1986). It is these concerns that this book addresses. The current work therefore proposes to investigate the impact of the World Bank funded Integrated Rural Development Programme (IRDP) on the two peasant villages in southeast Nigeria. Given the current controversies surrounding the World Bank's involvement in Third World agriculture (Beckman, 1981), the study of this involvement becomes more urgent.

Review of Literature

Increasing numbers of sociologists, and scholars in other related disciplines, are concerned about the deteriorating agrarian conditions in the Third World. In Africa, this decline has reached an unmanageable magnitude. There are diverse opinions as to the reasons behind this rapid decline. Some development experts have attributed the crisis of agrarian transformation in Africa to the extremely hostile environment, and to unpredictable climatic conditions (FAO, 1976; World Bank, 1989). Others like Theodore Schultz (1976) have sought explanations in the nature of incentives made available to peasant farmers. Similarly, neo-classical economists (Bates, 1976; Gallaher, 1991) blame the states in the Third World for the crisis of agriculture. Gallaher argues that the states in these formations demand payment for resources over and above what is necessary to get the resources to perform its function. This often discourages foreign participation in agricultural activities because of lack of profit incentives.

Lipton (1976) attributes Third World rural decline to the urban bias policies of the post-colonial states. Economic policies of the new states in the Third World, Lipton argues, often favoured the urban sector, since the policy makers aspire to finance rapid industrialization by withdrawing resources from the peasant economy. The withdrawal of resources from the rural economy, Lipton contends, often results in a pattern of uneven development which consequently obliterates the development efforts of these post-colonial states. The deliberate neglect of the rural economy, according to Lipton, led to a serious dislocation of the national economy. The result, Lipton argues, was the demographic surge on the urban centres by rural dwellers thereby complicating the efforts of policy makers.

Following Schultz (1976), Bates (1981) concedes that state intervention in Third World agriculture only distorts the markets, thereby denying the peasants "their fundamentally market rationality" (Bates, 1981:2). According to Bates, the lack of political legitimacy forced many Third World leaders to align themselves with the urban interest groups. In order to dissuade these urban interest groups from taking militant protest which might disrupt the process of national economic development, Bates argues that Third World leaders often embarked on urban biased economic policies which more often distort market rationality (Bates, 1981:3). Bates singles out the policy of food subsidies to urban workers by Third World governments, and also the practice of forced price control on rural produce. As a result, Bates continues, "by adopting policies that confound the operation of markets, Third World governments undercut the productive potentials of their farm populations" (Bates, 1981:2).

By Bates reckoning, African governments' intervention in agriculture, has the potential of distorting the market in addition to setting the limit on the probability of investment in agriculture. Peasant producers, discouraged by unfavorable market prices, Bates argues, could hardly take the sort of risk necessary to invest in production. The rational choice approach to agricultural development, popularized by Bates, raises more troubling questions. Aside from the ahistorical character of this argument, its free enterprise focus, some have argued, only reveals a bias towards capitalist paradigm that had informed agricultural development in industrial world (Watts, 1987).

This rational choice approach has come under severe criticisms from other scholars, most especially, radical scholars. For instance, Bretts points out that such rational choice focus on market rationality often ignore or gloss over the fact that there are other developmental models through which peasant agriculture could be transformed (Bretts, 1985). Besides, rational choice theorists also ignore the fact that state intervention in Third World agriculture dated back to the colonial era (Helleiner, 1968;Bates, 1974). As Bates (1976) himself had shown in his earlier study of peasant agriculture in Zambia, the contradiction between commercial agricultural production for export that was favoured by the colonial state, and peasants subsistence farming, accounted for the pattern of uneven development that characterized most of the Third World formations (Bates, 1974).

Indeed, several scholars have argued that commercial agriculture only served the economic interest of the colonial bourgeoisie, while impoverishing the peasant producers who were often forced to switch arable land for export crops (Williams, 1976; Hart, 1982). Secondly, state intervention in peasant production, as Helleiner (1966) argues, was the most effective means through which the colonial state and its successor elite could expropriate peasants' surplus. The implication of these arguments was that market forces have had very little relevance to Third World experience, given that state intervention in the economic process had been the norm rather than the exception (Beckman, 1985).

Henrique Cardoso (1973a) was among the first wave of Third World scholars who disagreed with the World Bank's views of its economic policies towards many Latin American countries. The tendency among the bank economists then was to blame the failure for their misinformed policies on Latin American governments, and on what they often dubbed as the "internal characteristics" of developing nations. For instance, during the sixties, the bank routinely focused upon the rapid rate of political democratization, and corruption among government officials, as important factors in the failure of the bank's economic policies. There are several reasons for the bank's failure in generating economic development in Latin America according to Cardoso. In a 1973 article, Cardoso argues that the bank's economic policies in Latin America failed primarily because of its internal contradictions, especially its inability to generate a model that was capable of taking cognizance of the particular historical experience, and the specificity of conditions of the Latin countries that adopted the bank's economic development model in the early sixties.

Dos Santos (1973) also observes that the bank's model which worked so well for Europe and Japan, only created dual economies for the majority of the countries in Latin America that adopted the bank's economic programme (Dos Santos, op.cited). The bank's agricultural policies, in particular, according to Dos

Santos (1973), only generated a disjunction between the urban and rural sectors of the national economy. The result, Dos Santos argues, was the generation of the phenomenon of "growth without development", and an economy characterized by dualism (Furtado, 1970; Frank, 1966; Dos Santos, 1973; Quijano:1977).

Rodolfo Stavenhagen (1973), a Mexican economist, also notes that the capitalist economic paradigm proposed by the World Bank for the developing nations was conceptualized, and based upon eighteenth century European historical experience and social conditions that could certainly not be reproduced today. For instance, capitalism developed and prospered in Europe, precisely because the European powers were able to annex colonies that served as a source of cheap labour and raw materials, as well as a ready market for its industrial goods.

Theoretical Perspectives on Rural Transformation

A. The Neo-classical Model

Until recently, agrarian transformation theories have been equally dominated by perspectives informed by the neo-classical economic model. The leading neo-classical theorists such as Arthur Lewis (1954), paid very little attention to the role of agriculture in economic development. In his famous article, "Economic Development with Unlimited Labor Supply", Lewis argues that the capitalist industrial sector is the key to economic development. He identified two sectors within the national economy; the capitalist sector with self reproducible capital, and the indigenous non-capitalist sector dominated by subsistence farming. According to Lewis's model, "expansion in the capitalist sector continues until earnings in the two sectors were equated at which point a dual-sector is no longer relevant; growth proceeded in one sector like the neo-classical model." (Eicher, C.K. et al.,1990:5). This marginalization of the agricultural sector in national development, by neo-classical theorists, set the tune for the modernization paradigm for development in the 1950s and 1960s.

Raul Presbisch, an economist working at the Economic Commission for Latin America (ECLA), contends that growth based on agricultural exports was very limited compared to those generated by the export of manufactured goods (Presbisch, 1959, 1981). Presbisch proposed that developing nations should set their goals towards import substitution of manufactured goods rather than agricultural produce. The assumption here is that the choice of import substitution policy will lead to a breakthrough in industry, which eventually will free labour from the rural sector, setting in motion a process of economic development reminiscent of the Western experience.

Hirschman's research, in the early 1950s, supports the position of the ECLA economists on import substitution. Hirschman, like Presbisch, suggests that investment in industry should take priority over all other sectors, because growth in industry would surely lead to a broadly based rapid growth of the economy, more than it would have been, were investment to be concentrated in agriculture (Hirschman, 1958).

These neo-classical views were challenged by Jorgenson (1961) who recognized the interdependence, or linkage, between agricultural and industrial growth. Jorgenson contends that growth in non-farm employment sectors depended, to a large extent, on the rate of growth in agricultural surplus (Eicher, C.K. et al. 1990:6). Jorgenson points out that there should be equilibrium in investment between the agricultural and the industrial sectors. He notes that, in the long-run, agriculture's share of investment will decline as agricultural production becomes more mechanized, and more and more farm labour is released for employment in the non-farm sector of the economy. Ranis (1964) proposed a middle ground to Lewis's two sectors' model and Jorgenson's equilibrium thesis. According to Ranis, in order to avoid "falling into low equilibrium trap in the early stages of development, a country probably needed to make some net investment in agriculture to accelerate growth of its agricultural surplus." (Eicher, et.al.,1990:6). This surplus would in turn, Ranis argues, be invested in industry thereby accelerating the process of industrialization.

By the sixties, the diffusion model of rural development became more and more popular amongst development experts. However by the seventies, the crisis of agrarian transformation had intensified in much of the developing world. This situation led to a re-examination of the diffusion model inspired by the neo-classical perspective. As Eicher and Staatz note:

> During the 1950s the approach of European and North American agricultural economists to development was colored by the historical experiences of their own countries, and by their own training in the current theories of economic development. For example, most Western agricultural economists working on problems of the Third World believed that the problem of rural surplus labor could be resolved by transferring "excess" rural workers to urban industry. It was also widely assumed that Western agricultural advisers could directly

transfer agricultural technology and models of agricultural extension from high-income countries to the Third World (Eicher, C.K. et al., 1990:7).

Eicher and others also suggest that the diffusion model was pushed during the cold war era to prevent any revolutionary approach to rural transformation in the Third World (Eicher, et al. 1990:8). The apparent failure of the neo-classical model inspired a new paradigm informed by the political economy approach to economic analysis.

B. The Political Economy Model

Paul Baran's work in the early 1950s consistently challenged the neo-classical modernization model of development. Inspired by the works of Lenin and Karl Kautsky on agriculture, Baran argues that agrarian transformation in the Third World requires a revolutionary re-arrangement of their social structures, while recognizing the fact, like the neo-classical theorists, that smallholder farming was hardly the solution to problems of agrarian decay in the Third World. Contrary to the generally held belief in development circles, Baran saw capitalism as part of the problem. Capitalism, Baran contends, often complicates the efforts of equity based transformation in the Third World (Baran, 1952).

Baran's critique of the neo-classical perspective inspired several radical researches in the late 1960s and 1970s. In particular, younger economists at the ECLA like Frank (1966), Furtado (1973), and Dos Santos (1972), began to apply the political economy and dependency model to the understanding of under-development in the Third World. These scholars saw underdevelopment, unlike modernization theorists, not as a stage in the process of economic development, but as a peculiar condition brought about by capitalism's incursion into Third World economy. This is as a result of historical condition of dependence, the radical scholars argued, created by the western metropolitan powers. Colonialism, these authors argue, was a precursor to this peculiar situation of dependence (Frank, 1966).

Emmanuel (1972) identifies the problem as one of unequal exchange between the periphery of the world economy and the Western metropolis. He argues that unequal exchange between the underdeveloped countries and the Western nations arose out of "the maintenance of depressed wage rates and the use of monopoly power by industrial nations to turn the terms of trade against the Third World" (Eicher et al., 1990:11). Emmanuel recommends that Third World nations unite and create their own cartels to break the Western monopoly of the world market.

In a 1978 article, Lewis disagrees with Emmanuel's thesis of unequal exchange. Lewis argues, in contradistinction to Emmanuel's thesis, that unequal exchange in the global economy arose not because of the persistence of colonial dependence and monopolistic practices by the West, but because of the failure of the Third World countries to invest adequately in their internal production (Lewis, 1978). Whatever the strength of their arguments, the inability of dependency theorists to analyse Third World class structure, tend to weaken the analytic value of their model in our understanding of the persistence of economic backwardness in the Third World.

C. The Modes of Production Model

The failure of the world system and dependency theories in providing an analysis of the class structure of Third World formations led to a new theoretical perspective which now came to be known as the modes of production school. This school recognizes the fact that the dependency theory represents a valid critique of the neo-classical modernization school of thought. However, the modes of production scholars argue that dependency theory remains essentially within the modernization problematic.

Taking a different view of dependency, Taylor (1976) contends that the inability of the centre-periphery paradigm to transform the positivism, and teleology within the modernization perspective, renders this paradigm an inadequate tool of analysis in terms of analysing structures of dependence and underdevelopment in the periphery of the world economy. In a sense, Taylor's critique of the dependency and world system schools, as we shall show later, centres around the crucial fact that both schools lack a coherent theoretical and analytical model that would demonstrate how capitalist mode of production uses non-capitalist systems in realizing and ensuring its own "expanded reproduction".

In the main, the modes of production school of thought addresses the question of the various forms of articulation within the global capitalist mode of production as a crucial step in understanding how a particular form of articulation results in an uneven development that the current global capitalist economy represents. By articulation, the mode of production scholars mean a structured relation between the capitalist modes of production and the non-capitalist sectors. The modes of production school tries to understand how these articulations shape the pattern of capitalist development on the global scale (Taylor, 1976; Amin, 1978). According to the modes of production thesis, the "reproductive needs" of capital is satisfied by the maintenance of non-capitalist sectors within the global system of production (Taylor, 1976). In other words, by retaining the pre-capitalist modes in its original forms (including the preservation of its ideological purity), the capitalist mode of production is able to exploit these modes to meet the conditions of its own reproduction. This ontological conception of capitalist reproduction itself creates more problems for the modes of production scholars, Taylor in particular, since it makes empirical verification of which relations or articulations are intended to secure the "reproductive needs" of capital a very difficult exercise.

The Argentinean sociologist, Earnesto Laclau (1976) points to the confusion which often arose in our understanding of the processes of economic development in the Third World. This problem arose from the readiness of economists and sociologists alike to confuse different and separate levels of analysis. By confusing an economic system with the modes of production, Laclau contends, sociologists often gloss over an important component which may render our analysis inappropriate (Laclau, 1976). For Laclau, economic system comprises of different modes of production and their interconnections. The modes of production on the other hand, according to Laclau, defines a specific articulation between the relations of production (mode of surplus appropriation), and forces of production (i.e. mode of expropriation of nature) (Laclau, 1971:37-8).

In focusing on the economic system as the unit of analysis, Laclau argues, the dependency school and the world system theorists, confused contradictions which are essentially at the level of the mode of production as contradictions generated by the system of capitalist production. As a result, Laclau continues, the dualism between the advanced capitalist West and the Third World is seen as the defining characteristics of Third World underdevelopment. Instead, Laclau sees these contradictions as the manifestation of the effects of articulation of the global capitalist mode of production with different non-capitalist modes, and the specific pattern of accumulation defined by the relations among the different modes of production within the global economy.

By conceiving of economic systems as combinations of different modes of production, the argument goes, we would be able to specify how their

26

articulations result in the development of one sector of the global economy, and the "underdevelopment" of others (Taylor, 1976; Laclau, 1976). The implication of this conclusion by the modes of production scholars is that we should be able to analyze the World Bank's agricultural policies (IRDPs) in the Third World as an important process in the global pattern of accumulation. In so far as the modes of production thesis is concerned, the primary function of the World Bank agricultural policies in the Third World would be to facilitate the process of integration of these formations into the global capitalist economy (Wallerstein, 1986; Taylor, 1976).

This contention precludes the alternative thesis that the World Bank involvement in Third World agriculture promotes the basis for autonomous development of the economies of these formations. This is the crucial theoretical distinction between the supporters of the ADPs and those who had consistently opposed them.

Trends in the 1980s

Despite the theoretical rigour of the modes of production school, it has been very difficult to use this model for concrete research. Increasingly, researchers are turning to new models that focus on income distribution and employment in the rural sectors of the economy. One such model, which continues to gain widespread support in the 1980s and 1990 is the "Growth with Equity Model". The model criticizes the neo-classical diffusion model for focusing exclusively on peasants' productivity and ignoring other indicators such as diets, nutrition and income gap between different strata of the rural population. Similarly, the "Growth with Equity" model has also challenged the diffusion fallacy implicit in the neo-classical model. For instance, several studies commissioned by the World Bank (cf. Lele Uma and Agarwal, 1989), concluded that, where the diffusion model worked in the Third World, the "benefits of economic growth were not trickling down to the poor, and that frequently, the income gap between the rich and poor was widening. Even where the incomes of the poor were rising, often they were rising so slowly that the poor would not be able to afford decent diets or housing for at least another generation". (Eicher, et al. 1990:13).

While the World Bank's agricultural policies continue to emphasize projects that target rich peasants as the last hope of capitalist agriculture in the Third World, its policies are gradually being influenced by the "equity with growth model" as we shall show towards the end of this book. To this end, the

27

bank has begun to expand the measures of success of its programme to include other factors beyond peasants' productivity.

We now take a brief look at the role of the World Bank in Third World agricultural development as a conclusion to this chapter. The bank continues to play this role because of its monopoly of development resources, and because of its traditional role of organizing the global capitalist economy.

The World Bank, IRDPs and ADPs

Integrated Rural Development Projects (IRDPs), were first introduced in south East Asia. The aim of the IRDPs was to improve agricultural production in the Third World. The goal is to improve crop yields by encouraging peasant farmers to use fertilizers, and to adopt modern technology. The programme was later extended to Africa, especially Nigeria, where it was adopted as Agricultural Development Projects (ADPs). The ADP also has as its primary focus, the replacement of peasant farming by capitalist agriculture (Williams, 1986). In Africa, especially Nigeria, the ADPs were extended to include massive irrigation projects, pastoral farming, animal husbandry and multinational experimental farms. The World Bank provided financial and technical advice to developing countries qualifying for the programme, while technical inputs, in the form of heavy agricultural tools, are provided by western nations as part of a comprehensive development aid package.

The results of the IRDPs and ADPs are very difficult to evaluate, partly because of the bank's refusal to allow independent study of these farms, and also because some of the projects are too young for an objective appraisal study. However, studies commissioned by the World Bank were often full of praise, while those by independent researchers tended to draw negative reviews (Beckman, 1985; Williams, 1987). As was the case in the past when the bank openly acknowledged failure of its IRDPs, it nevertheless often blamed the developing countries (World Bank: Sub-Saharan Africa 1989).

However, many economists at the Economic Commission for Africa (ECA) have challenged the bank's analysis of the failure of its economic policies in Africa. In its latest report, *Economic Report on Africa* (1990), the ECA blamed external factors (including the World Bank economic policies in Africa) for the persisting economic crisis and problems of transformation in Africa. The report written by not so radical economists at the ECLA was suspicious of the involvement of foreign multinationals in African development. It also expressed pessimism with regards to the question of Africa's economic recovery when it states thus:

> The general deterioration in the African economic and social conditions is a direct outcome of the worsening domestic development setting and the extremely unfavorable external economic and financial environment. The persistence of the crisis, with its relentless aggravation, has indeed convinced all genuine friends of Africa that the policy framework for grappling with the economic and social crisis has not always been adequate and often is inappropriate (ECA report, 1990).

The ECA report reflects the feeling of many African governments, most of whom have little beyond dependency and a ruined economy to show to their people for their commitment to the World Bank induced economic programme, which they have adopted for more than three decades. While it is premature to comment on the ECA report, the need to evaluate these projects becomes more urgent due to the harshness of conditions which Africa has witnessed in the past five years as Table 2.1 below shows. The embarrassing decline in agricultural production for most independent African states during the period 1974 to 1984 reveals a pattern of economic decay throughout black Africa. This period was chosen because it was the most disastrous period in terms of worsening food crisis in a continent that has since repeated famines and regular crop failure. In the particular case of Nigeria, the period in review, as was mentioned above, also coincided with the accelerated industrialization programme of the Nigerian state during which the state substituted internally generated growth with import substitution creating a heavy drain on foreign earnings that could have gone into rural development.

This general decline in food production relative to population growth in most postcolonial African states has been blamed on the kind of economic policies these states pursued immediately after decolonization. In addition to this, inadequate birth control, especially in the rural areas produced population explosion which put burdens on the planning process. As is well known, economic planning could only be achieved based on reliable census data, and for most African states, these data where available are extremely unreliable. In the case of Nigeria, efforts to conduct a national census have been marred by political difficulties due to suspicion of the population as to how such data will be put into use. Besides this general suspicion, military rulers and politicians have also used census data for selfish purposes.

Table 2.1: Selected African Countries: Population and Food Production per Capita, 1974-84

Country	Population mid-1984 and % increase 1973-84 (millions)	Growth in food production (1974/6 baseline)
Algeria	21.2 (3.1)	79 (-21%)
Beni	3.9 (2.8)	97 (- 3%)
Botswana	0 .1 (2.8)	61 (-39%)
Burkina Faso	6.6 (1.8)	94 (- 6%)
Cameroon	9.9 (3.1)	83 (-17%)
Congo	1.8 (3.1)	96 (- 4%)
Cot d'Ivoire	9.9 (4.5)	110 (10%)
Egypt	45.9 (2.6)	91 (0%)
Ghana	12.3 (2.6)	73 (-27%)
Guinea	5.9 (2.0)	93 (- 7%)
Kenya	19.6 (4.0)	82 (-18%)
Liberia	2.1 (3.3)	91 (- 9%)
Libya	3.5 (4.1)	94 (- 6%)
Madagascar	9.9 (2.8)	89 (-11%)
Malawi	6.8 (3.1)	100 (0%)
Mali	7.3 (2.6)	101 (1%)
Mauritania	1.7 (2.1)	95 (- 5%)
Morocco	21.4 (2.4)	91 (- 9%)
Niger	6.2 (3.0)	113 (13%)
Nigeria	96.5 (2.8)	96 (- 4%)
Senegal	6.4 (2.8)	66 (-36%)
Sierra Leone	3.7 (2.1)	95 (- 5%)
Sudan	1.3 (2.9)	93 (- 7%)
Tanzania	21.5 (3.4)	100 (0%)
Togo	2.9 (2.8)	92 (- 8%)
Tunisia	7.0 (2.4)	84 (-16%)

Table 2.1 (con't)

Country	Population mid-1984 and % increase 1973-84 (millions)	Growth in food production (1974/76 baseline)
Uganda	15.0 (3.2)	98 (- 2%)
Zaire	29.7 (3.0)	92 (- 8%)
Zambia	6.4 (3.2)	74 (-26%)
Zimbabwe	8.1 (3.2)	69 (-31%)

Source: Adapted from World Bank Development
Report, 1986. Washington, D.C.

As was mentioned earlier in this section, the deterioration in economic conditions throughout Africa, particularly the rapidly declining agricultural production, led to the adoption of the World Bank's agricultural assistance programme in sub-Sahara Africa. In Nigeria for example, there are a number of these projects, none of which has been thoroughly investigated. It is thus the objective of this work to examine some of these projects in light of the rapid deterioration of the Nigerian economy and the dwindling of resources from crude petroleum. In the next chapter, we describe the project area where data for this current work were collected.

3 Agrarian Crisis in Nigeria

Section I: Trends in Agrarian Decline

Prior to independence in 1960, agrarian production was the backbone of the economy with a self sufficiency in food production. This sufficiency in food, and export related production, could be explained by the government concern for rural production as the sole source of state revenue. For instance, during the 1954-64 fiscal year, the food import bill amounted to less than 10 percent of the total import bill. However, by the late seventies agriculture was beginning to lose its importance as the sole source of state income. By then the food import bill had jumped to 18 percent of total import bill (Central Bank of Nigeria reports, 1950-65).

By the end of the sixties, agricultural exports had declined to little less than six percent of total export from a peak of 86 percent in the years leading to independence (Turner and Badru, 1985). The crude petroleum boom of the early 1970s contributed to the relative neglect of the agricultural sector of the economy. This general decline in agrarian production can be seen in the decreasing pattern of land area under agricultural production, and increasing grain imports such as wheat and rice. This period of decline also coincided with increasing lack of concern by state bureaucrats for rural production since the contribution of agriculture to gross national produce was becoming more and more marginal.

The policy of import substitution industrialization, adopted in the seventies by the Nigerian state, had as its underlying principle a gradual transformation of rural production which would be sparked by rapid development in the industrial sector of the economy. If things worked well, as it did in the European experience, development in heavy industry would provide the necessary technology for a massive mechanization of peasants' production. As more labour is released from rural production, the argument goes, the surplus labour released will be automatically picked up in the heavy industry sector of the economy.

This was never the case, import substitution industrialization in Nigeria only led to the collapse of rural production. The tables in the following pages document the sharp decline in agricultural production since independent statehood was achieved.

Table 3.1: Total Land Area Under Cultivation for Sixteen Major Crops ('000 ha.)

Year	Total Land Under Cultivation
1965/66	20,377
1966/67	16,196
1967/68	18,345
1968/69	18,694
1969/70	22,944
1970/71	20,336
1971/72	15,489
1972/73	19,929
1973/74	16,816
1974/75	14,939
1976/77	15,009
1977/78	11,057
1978/79	9,507
1979/80	8,626
1980/81	9,648

Source: Federal Ministry of Agriculture,
Department of Agricultural Planning,
Lagos, Nigeria, 1982.

33

Table 3.2: Share of Agriculture in Gross Domestic Product

Year	Total All Sectors (N.million)	Agriculture Sector (N.million)	% of Total
1953	1,623.2	1,059.2	65.25
1954	1,744.2	1,115.6	63.96
1955	1,790.4	1,144.6	63.93
1956	1,747.4	1,103.6	63.16
1957	1,820.0	1,130.4	62.11
1958	1,800.0	1,239.8	68.88
1959	1,877.0	1,226.0	65.32
1960	1,962.6	1,280.0	65.22
1961	2,247.4	1,414.6	62.94
1962	2,359.6	1,453.2	61.59
1963	2,597.6	1,605.8	61.82
1964	2,745.8	1,673.8	60.96
1965	2,894.4	1,676.4	57.92
1966	3,110.0	1,691.8	54.39
1967	3,374.8	1,855.0	54.97
1968	2,752.6	1,527.8	55.50
1969	2,656.2	1,415.2	53.28
1970	3,549.3	1,711.2	48.23
1971	5,281.1	2,576.4	48.49
1972	6,650.9	3,033.7	45.61
1973	7,187.5	3,092.7	43.03
1974	12,118.0	3,352.1	27.66
1975	16,462.8	3,943.0	23.95
1976	19,437.7	4,579.5	23.56
1977	23,826.0	4,898.3	20.56
1978	26,758.5	5,143.4	19.22
1979	27,370.2	5,389.1	19.69
1980	31,424.7	5,656.8	18.00

Source: Federal Ministry of Agriculture,
Information Bulletin on Agriculture, 1984, p.12.
Reproduced from Iyegha, D.A; 1988, p.32.

**Table 3.3: Actual Food Importation
in Nigeria, 1964-84**

Year	Food	Vegetable oil and fat
1964	41.24	0.26
1965	46.08	0.35
1966	51.57	0.37
1967	42.56	0.60
1968	28.39	0.58
1969	41.73	0.38
1970	57.69	0.85
1971	87.91	0.72
1972	95.10	1.06
1973	126.26	1.39
1974	154.76	3.57
1975	297.86	8.92
1976	440.93	24.69
1977	736.46	47.01
1978	1,027.11	81.26
1979	952.40	97.99
1980	1,049.05	115.00
1981	1,820.22	128.74
1982	1,642.265	151.37
1983	1,296.71	105.56
1984	843.25	101.76

Source: Federal Office of Statistics,
Abstract of Statistics and Trade Summary
Lagos, Nigeria. Reproduced from
Igheha:1988, p.37.

Table 3.4: Rice Production and Importation in Nigeria, 1970-79

Yr.	Local (tons)	Importation (tons)	Total (tons)	Import Bill (N.Million)
1970	345,000	1,700	346,700	1.14
1971	383,000	300	383,000	0.05
1972	447,000	5,900	452,000	0.99
1973	487,000	1,100	488,000	0.27
1974	525,000	4,000	529,000	1.50
1975	515,000	6,700	521,000	2.38
1976	534,000	45,000	579,00 0	20.14
1977	667,000	413,000	1,080,000	154.94
1978	695,000	770,000	1,465,000	194.76
1979	850,000	700,000	1,530,000	121.71

Source: Reproduced from Aribisala:1983, p.8.

While the tables above show a dramatic increase in stable food importation, there was also a steady decline in the production of some export crops which previously had been vital to the national economy. Table 3.5 below shows the decline of some selected export crops especially cocoa and groundnuts, crops in which Nigeria had been a leading exporter.

Table 3.5: Production of Principal Agricultural Export Commodities (000 tons), 1965-81

Year	Cocoa	Palm oil	Peanut	Cotton	Beni-seed
1966/67	263	32	1185	112	23
1967/68	234	4	1091	209	16
1968/69	185	-	1269	446	-
1969/70	224	na	1292	372	16
1970/71	308	na	1581	357	22
1971/72	254	na	1380	425	21
1972/73	241	na	1350	105	4
1973/74	-	na	877	85	4

Table 3.5 (cont')

Table 3.5: Production of Principal Agricultural Export Commodities (000 tons), 1965-81

Year	Cocoa	Palm oil	Peanut	Cotton	Beni-seed
1974/75	214	na	1935	481	15
1975/76	-	na	458	311	15
1976/77	165	-	460	294	14
1977/78	-	na	603	269	9
1978/79	137	na	701	212	15
1979/80	-	na	453	125	7
1980/81	155	na	675	77	2

Source: Iyegha, D.A. 1988:38.

By the 1980s, the shift in state policy from agrarian based development to one that emphasized rapid industrialization was accompanied by a shift in attitude and taste. Increasingly, migration from the rural areas to the seemingly booming urban centres led to severe shortages in the agricultural sector of the economy further exacerbating the food crisis. The decision to pursue urban based development strategy could be seen most clearly in the discriminatory pattern of investment between the urban and the rural sectors of the economy. Sectoral allocation began to favour the non-agricultural sector of economy especially infrastructural development.

Between 1962 and 1968, there was 83.6 percent differential in actual sectoral investment between rural and urban sectors of the economy. This situation worsened progressively throughout the eighties. In many cases, sectoral investments in agriculture were often made by foreign multinationals such as Lever Brothers. These investments were usually restricted to export crop production or to production of crops that were used locally by these multinationals in their day to day operations.

Even investments in cattle production were also restricted to industries exporting beef abroad or to neighbouring West African countries where such demands for beef existed. At the time, export crop production became so attractive that members of the Nigerian bourgeoisie, and army officers moved huge amounts of capital to this sector. Ironically, those "gentlemen" farmers, as they were known, actually relied on food importation for their day to day survival even when they had the means to produce food.

Table 3.6: Distribution of Public Sector Investment 1965-85 (percent)

	1962-68		1970-74		1975-80		1981-85	
	p	a	p	a	p	a	p	a
Agric.	13.6	7.7	9.4	9.8	6.7	7.2	12.5	-
Non-.	86.4	92.3	90.6	90.2	93.3	92.8	87.5	-

agric. a= actual; b=planned capital allocation

Source: Federal Republic of Nigeria, National Development Plans of Nigeria, 1962-85.

Behind this shift in state policy was the untested hypothesis that once industrialization is achieved, the rural sector would in no time be transformed. As Chinzea observes:

> Agricultural policy in neo-colonial epoch in Nigeria is not markedly different from the colonial approach. The gist of the whole approach to agriculture is the accelerated investment and capitalization of agricultural production. The aim is to progressively reduce the agricultural population so as to create labor for industry (Chinzea, 1985:55).

Teresa Turner (1980), and other scholars like Claude Ake (1985) and Bade Onimade (1982) argued that the Nigerian state strategy of import substitution industrialization could not produce the desired result partly because of the peculiar incorporation of the Nigerian economy into the world system and the pervasiveness of graft and corruption among state officials. Indeed, it was during this phase of accelerated industrialization that foreign multinationals plundered the economy in collaboration with state bureaucrats. Despite its glaring failure, this model of crude sponsored industrialization was pursued into the eighties on the insistence of the Nigerian neo-classical economists, who dominated state bureaucracy. This marked the beginning of a new era in terms of national economic development direction.

The collapse of the national economy by the early eighties led the state officials and policy makers to embark on a strategy of rapid agricultural revitalization. In a sense, the policy change reflects the indirect acceptance by the Nigerian state of the failure of its industrialization programme. The need to concentrate on food production became the new cornerstone of the military administrators (Badru, 1984; Ihimodu, 1991). In 1975, a national food programme was sponsored by the administration of the military dictator General Obasanjo. This new programme was sarcastically dubbed "Operation Feed the Nation" (OFN). The programme aimed at improving peasant production through the use of fertilizers, and the introduction of high yielding hybrid crops. Several billions of naira were committed to the programme. As we shall show in the later part of this chapter, funding for the new programme did not actually go to the peasants, but into pockets and bank accounts of senior military officers and state bureaucrats (Turner and Badru, 1985).

In 1978, the military Head of State, General Obasanjo, summoned the National Economic Council charging it with the responsibility of finding a permanent solution to the agrarian crisis. The council concluded that the rural crisis was primarily caused by poor organization of peasant agriculture, backwardness and stone age technology, the parochial attitudes of peasant producers, and the small size of peasant farms among other things (Adedeji, 1989). The council thus recommended the displacement of peasant farming by capitalist agriculture. It also called for the development within the ranks of the peasants, of capitalist farmers and entrepreneurs who would seize the advantage offered by the new investment in agriculture.

These new policy recommendations led to the launching of a new programme - the Green Revolution. This programme was no different from its predecessor, Operation Feed the Nation, except that the budget for its execution was nearly twice as much. The major beneficiaries, as we shall point out later in this chapter, were members of the military, who sought new careers in farming (Turner and Badru, 1985).

As it turned out, the Green Revolution formed the basis for a new pattern of accumulation by the ruling elite. But this accumulation did not lead to a transformation of the rural economy. The Green Revolution, as we argue below, only accelerated the process of rural decline partly because of poor execution and corruption by bureaucrats, petty state and local government officials, and high level military officers (Turner and Badru, 1985). The failure of both the OFN and GR led the new military leadership to proceed to adopt the Integrated Rural Development Project (IRDP) as a new model for rural transformation.

ADPs: The Controversies

In following the recommendations of the 1978 presidential commission on the food crisis, the Nigerian State set up a Food Strategies Commission, comprising Nigerian and World Bank officials. It recommended the adoption of Agricultural Development Projects with funding coming from the World Bank. Like the Integrated Rural Development Projects (IRDPs), the ADPs are also grounded in the modernization paradigm of agrarian transformation. The programme envisaged a systematic replacement of peasants' mode of production by capitalist agriculture. It called for private and foreign capital in agriculture, with the state limiting its role to the provision of infrastructure in the form of feeder roads to rural areas. In order to facilitate the implementation of the programme, the Nigerian government abrogated a long-standing law that put a ceiling of 40 percent to multinational corporations' participation in agriculture.

Earlier on, three pilot projects were established in 1976 in Sokoto, Baauchi, and Kaduna in northern Nigeria. The initial emphasis of these pilot projects was the development of irrigation through the use of water dams. This ambitious programme required huge amounts of funding, which could only come from international finance institutions. At the Bakolori dam, for example, the execution price of the dam was so high that the original cost of the project was upgraded to three times its original cost (Beckman, 1985). The projects also demanded large scale social transformation. One of the social costs of the programme is mass displacement of farmers in the project area. In many cases many peasants were forcefully removed by the state without concrete plans for their resettlement. In fact, the prospect of homelessness among displaced farmers often led to resentment and resistance as was the case with the Bakolori. Frequent blockade of the project sites was one way peasant farmers registered their protest with the state.

Despite the ambivalent results of the three pilot projects (cf. Berg's report, 1981), and against the background of militant peasants' reaction against land acquisition for the projects, the military government pressed ahead for the establishment of similar ADPs nationwide (Beckman, 1985; Abdullahi, 1983;

Berg Report 1981). One interesting observation is that the period the World Bank was pressing for the adoption of the ADPs also coincided with the phase of increased IMF agricultural loans to the Nigerian state (Onimade, 1989). This raises the question of whether the World Bank was really concerned with rural transformation in Nigeria, or simply interested in advancing economic opportunities for foreign multinationals involved in agro-business in the country. As Beckman argues, the expansion of the ADPs provided the opportunity for multinational corporations that supply agricultural equipments to expand their Nigerian market (Beckman, 1985).

In the Bakolori project, Beckman (1985) showed that inputs were supplied by Caterpillar International and Fiat, the largest Italian automobile corporation. It is interesting to note that Fiat has a long standing affiliation with the United Nations' agency "Food and Agricultural Organization" (FAO) which is responsible for the design of the bank's projects worldwide. Another Italian company, partly controlled by Fiat, handled the construction of the damn at Bakolori. This network of cooperation between multinational corporations and international finance institutions has also been one area of controversy by scholars who followed agrarian development in Nigeria (Williams, 1988; Beckman, 1985). The collaboration between multinationals and the bank often raised puzzling questions for scholars as Beckman (1985) revealed in the study of the Bakolori project in northern Nigeria.

This contentious issue of multinationals' dominance of the ADPs apart, the question of stratification within the peasantry has also been challenged. In the particular experience of Nigeria, the ADPs target the middle and upper strata of the peasantry as possible candidates for capitalist agriculture (Williams, 1988; Dunmoye, 1982). It has been shown (Beckman, 1985) that the major beneficiaries of the ADPs are capitalist farmers drawn from the ranks of retired army officers and civil servants who are generally absentee landlords (Turner and Badru, 1985). Between the middle and upper peasantry, they compete for resources in the form of heavy machinery and hybrid seeds, while the poor peasants are usually left out. In fact, the World Bank was very clear in terms of its objectives, when it stated that the aim of ADPs in Sub-Sahara Africa is to promote capitalist farmers through:

> ...technological development, and making agriculture attractive to private investors, by attending to the needs of the large farmers, and smallholder groups who displayed sufficient business acumen to

advance beyond the level of basic husbandry and crop yield during the implementation period (World Bank report; 1976).

This, in a nutshell, is the cardinal objective of the bank's intervention in Third World peasant agriculture. What this research uncovered is that the project's administrators were more preoccupied with the creation of a class of capitalist farmers, and lost sight of the question of rural poverty. By creating this stratum, the project officials hoped to build a viable capitalist agricultural structure geared towards export production. The underlying principle is that farmers would be better off growing export crops, where they are more competitive. This, to say the least, is absurd in a country where the majority of the population live off the land, and where industrial production is next to nothing. One explanation for this absurd recommendation is that the bank was simply interested in financing production that would bring in foreign currency, which in turn would allow the country to repay its debts. Where this practice had been adopted, the end result is widespread food shortages, and imported foods are normally too expensive for farmers to purchase. For example in the case of the Ethiopian famine of the mid eighties, there was not only a surplus in grain production for export, the country actually increased its export earnings based on grain exportation abroad while the entire country starved to death. This aspect of the programme will be discussed fully in the concluding chapter.

Section II: Brief History of National Planning in Nigeria

I. Politics and Agriculture: Agricultural Revitalization Efforts of the Nigerian State

The concern of the Nigerian state immediately after independence, like its predecessor, was on how to transform peasant smallholder agriculture in the direction that would boost its productivity. This concern for rural production until crude petroleum became crucial to state revenue, arose out of the need to extract more surplus from rural producers to finance state operations. In order to finance the growing bureaucracy, since the government is the sole employer of labour, National Plans became an effective instrument of exploiting peasants' surplus produce. However, national planning dated back to the colonial era. For example, the first bold effort to control and organize peasant production was contained in the "Public Land Acquisition Ordinance" of 1917 which gave the colonial government the exclusive right to acquire native land for public purposes. This notorious land acquisition ordinance was soon followed by an even bolder ordinance - "Nigerian Town and Country Planning Ordinance" of 1946. This ordinance empowered the colonial governor to acquire tribal land in southern Nigeria without compensation (Olatunbosun, 1968, 2). Throughout the colony, similar ordinances were passed empowering colonial administrators to seize communally owned land, and pass rights of ownership and use to the colonial governors. The Land and Natives Rights Ordinance empowered the colonial governor and other colonial provincial officials to administer land for commercial and public use purposes. The same ordinance also imposed tenancy fees on land occupied and cultivated by native Nigerians (Iyegha, 1988:98). The overall goal of these ordinances, as Iyegah points out, was to encourage the penetration of capitalist agriculture in the rural sector (Iyegha, 1988:98-106).

This pattern of encroachment of peasants and communally owned land continued after political independence. Post-colonial nationalist government pursued exactly the same strategy of displacing smallholder farmers in favour of capitalist agriculture. In a scholarly paper, a Nigerian social scientist, David Iyegah notes the continuity in postcolonial agricultural policy of the state thus:

> The post-colonial leaders who took over didn't change any of the rules, but promoted them to their own advantage, and to the ultimate detriment of the population.. In pursuit of their priority of export crop production, the regional governments of the First Republic, through their development Corporations, established cocoa, palm oil, rubber, and coconut plantations, especially in the then three southern regions. In addition, farm settlements were founded, the aim of which was not only to increase cash crop production, but also to transform peasant farming into capitalist farming (Iyegha, 1988:99).

In the old western region for instance, not less than 45 percent plantations and agricultural settlement schemes were set up covering 34,000 acres of peasants' land. Similarly, in the former eastern Nigeria, large plantations of average size of between 400-600 acres each, were established for the purpose of growing rubber and oil palm for export (Ake, 1985:62). Ironically, these attempts to replace smallholder farming by large scale capitalist farms did not work as anticipated by state bureaucrats. Except for rubber and oil palm plantations in the south east, it has been shown that almost all the export crops, especially cocoa, groundnut and Beni-seeds, could be produced more efficiently in the small plots owned and run by smallholder farmers (Clark, 1979).

Under pressure from the projects' administrators and crude petroleum multinationals, the Nigerian state was forced to resolve the question of land ownership once and for all. The boldest attempt yet to displace smallholder farmers came when the federal government introduced the Land Use Decree No. 6 of 1978. The decree, like the colonial ordinances of 1917 and 1946, vested land use, control and administration in the hands of state military governors. Even though this decree led to the appropriation of peasants from their land, it also undermined the traditional authority of clan chiefs who often used land allocation authority vested in them to enforce conformity amongst their subjects.

However, the decree by its design aimed at introducing mechanized large scale agriculture in the rural areas. For instance, in addition to the decree, the government also simultaneously relaxed regulations that previously banned foreign investors in the agricultural sector of the economy, while at the same time paying lip service to improving smallholder productivity (Ake, 1985:64). It is within this historic battle between the Nigerian state and peasant farmers that we situate the various agricultural programmes promoted by the World Bank in Nigeria. Since 1960, no less than five different agricultural experiments have been introduced with very little or no success. All the programmes were implicitly influenced by the diffusion model approach to agrarian transformation. The diffusion model aimed at spreading modern technology, and Western extension advice to smallholder farmers. As their names showed, all these programmes reflected the desperation of the Nigerian state.

II. National Food Acceleration Production Programme (NFAPP)

The first National Development Plan, covering the period 1962-68, was unveiled in January of 1962. The main focus of the plan was the agricultural sector. The plan provided for an investment of 2.3 billion U.S. dollars (see Federal Ministry of Information bulletin, 1962). The plan called for the establishment of "Farm Settlement Schemes" which would produce exclusively export crops. The plan barely ran its normal course before war broke out in 1967 resulting in its abandonment. The war was fought over unsatisfactory political arrangements that had been put into place by the British during de-colonization talks with the nationalist elites. The desire of the Igbos in southeast Nigeria to break away from the artificial union was based on perceived persecution and marginalization from civil administration at the federal level.

The war lasted for four gruelling years during which agricultural production almost came to a standstill. After the war in 1970, a second National Plan was presented. The main features of the plan were the reconstruction of war ravaged areas, and the rehabilitation of agricultural production, especially in areas that had been ravaged by war. A new campaign was embarked upon dubbed the National Food Acceleration Production Programme (NFAPP). The campaign was launched in 1974 by the military ruler, General Yakubu Gowon. The programme was put under the supervision of the Ministry of Finance with technical support coming from the International Institute for Tropical Agriculture (IITA) in Ibadan, western Nigeria. The objective of NAFPP was far less ambitious unlike the Farm Settlement programmes that were previously initiated. The emphasis was on improving peasants' productivity in staple food crops such as cassava, millet, yellow and white corn, yams, sorghum and coconuts.

Tangentially, the campaign also emphasized the introduction of modern farming equipments, and the diversification of crops planted by smallholder farmers on a single plot. The government distributed fertilizers and other farm inputs to farmers through the extension officers from the Ministry of Agriculture. But because of poor training and inadequate supervision from qualified personnel, most of the fertilizers distributed were either improperly applied, or simply left in the open sun to rot (Ogba, 1980:75). Despite the enormous investment in the NFAPP, agricultural production continued to stagnate (Tables 2.3 and 2.5). The military Head of State who introduced the NFAPP, General Gowon, was overthrown in 1975, and the new rulers declared the programme inappropriate, and a wasteful exercise. The new military administration came with a whole new set of development ideas which were expressed in the Third National Development Plan of 1975-80.

III. Operation Feed the Nation (OFN)

The third National Plan was introduced in May of 1976 with more fanfare than the previous ones. In the plan, 2.2 billion naira (2.3 billion U.S. dollars, 1976 exchange rate) was allocated specifically for rural development. The new agricultural programme favoured, by the new military officers, was tagged "Operation Feed the Nation" (OFN). The main emphasis of OFN was the mobilization of smallholder farmers for increased productivity. This was basically the same rhetoric contained in the two previous programmes. The difference was the media propaganda that accomplished the launching. The new military Head of State, General Olusegun Obasanjo, was shown on national television, dressed in a peasant's outfit, launching the programme in a desperate effort to appeal to all segments of society.

This time, the plan called for full participation of all strata of Nigerian society in the programme, and the focus was no longer on peasant farmers. Civil servants were encouraged to maintain a plot behind their homes to grow staple food stuffs. This was one way of bringing respectability to farming as a profession. In principle, OFN was designed to redress the inadequacies and short-falls of the previous programmes without a clear pretension for the smallholder farmers. The main objectives of the programmes were as follows:

a). To mobilize the nation towards self-sufficiency in food;

b). To encourage the section of population that relies on buying food to grow some of its own food;

c). To encourage general pride in agriculture through the realization that a nation that cannot feed itself cannot be proud;

d). To encourage balanced nutrition and thereby produce a healthy nation;

e). To discourage rural-urban migration by encouraging young people to remain on the land;

f). To produce agricultural surpluses for sale abroad to build foreign exchange reserves (Ogba, 1980:87-88).

The programme was divided into two phases. The first phase was launched on May 26, 1976. This was the propaganda phase, during which 27,000 university students were hired to "educate" peasant farmers as to the use of fertilizers, and the new farm equipment like tractors and combine harvesters which were made available to peasants' cooperatives nationwide.

The second phase was launched on June 2, 1977. It became obvious that a dose of revived state propaganda was necessary to move the campaign forward, because interest in the programme nationwide was beginning to wane. Several problems plagued the implementation and administration of the programme. Due to widespread corruption, inputs earmarked for the smallholder farmers were hijacked by middlemen who sold them at below the market prices back to unscrupulous state bureaucrats for a percentage of the cut.

It soon became clear that the agricultural loans designated to smallholder farmers were disbursed because of lack of collaterals. In addition to this, the lack of adequate communication between the state OFN directorate offices and the head office in Lagos also contributed to the failure of the programme. By 1979, it became clear that this programme, like its predecessors was nothing but another costly national joke.

Meanwhile, while the military was preparing for a hand over of power to an elected civilian government, the operation was turned into an avenue for looting state money by military personnel who were retiring from service. Several high level military and civil officials applied for agricultural loans that were specifically earmarked for peasant farmers. And because of their personal ties and close affiliation to the programmes, many of these officers simply retired with huge loans, and took new careers in farming. This class constitutes what are now known as "Gentlemen farmers" (Turner and Badru, 1985). Finally, when a new civilian government was voted in towards the end of 1979, incoming politicians saw the OFN as their last chance to make it in the game of Nigerian politics. Thus, the brief civilian rule of 1979-83, became a phase in Nigerian history of personal aggrandizement by corrupt politicians and officials.

IV. Green Revolution (GR)

The last of the agricultural revitalization programmes we will discuss in this chapter is the Green Revolution (GR). The programme was launched, to replace Operation Feed the Nation (OFN), in May of 1980 by the new civilian president Alhaji Shehu Shagari. The objective of this latest programme was " to create the means to meet the needs of the smallholder farmers and to spread the benefits of rural development" (Iyegah, 1988:105 citing Federal Ministry of Agriculture Bulletin, 1980). Contrary to the claims of the programme's executors to focus on the smallholder farmers, the programme actually ended up promoting large scale farming, favouring absentee landlords and retired military officers in terms of loan allocation (Turner and Badru, 1985). In fact, during the entire duration of the programme, several smallholder peasant farmers were displaced by new capitalist farmers and multinational corporations. These groups took advantage of the relaxation of land acquisition rules and participation by foreign investors, as contained in the Land Use Decree No. 6 of 1978, to convert the new programme to avenues for personal and corporate accumulation (Ake, 1985; Iyegha, 1989). The disjunction between the government's proclaimed intention and actual practice with regards to the execution of the GR was aptly put by Iyegha thus:

> Moreover, officials made public pronouncement that the smallholder would be helped in the program through subsidized fertilizer supplies, extension work, etc, on which the agricultural sector placed its hope because of the promise seen in the new civilian regime. But this Federal government also continued to promote large scale agriculture; and being concerned only about the supply of food for the urban consumers. It directed its attention from the smallholder and injected huge amounts of money into irrigation and the agricultural projects, some of which were already established (Iyegha, 1988:104).

Indeed, the Green Revolution, as Onimade and other critics have pointed out, provided the basis for competition over accumulation between urban based elites and corrupt politicians of the Second Republic (Onimade, 1983; Ake, 1985). The programme also facilitated the penetration of foreign capital into the rural areas more than the two previous programmes. The politicians in the ruling national party of Nigeria (NPN) used the GR to extend political patronage as Iyegha observes:

> The program (GR) which raised the hopes of the population turned out to be a political gimmick used by politicians to win support for their corrupt practices. It was therefore not surprising that the GR, whose institutional structure mirrored its predecessor, OFN, became an instrument by which peasants were exploited and alienated instead of mobilized (Iyegha, 1988:105).

By 1983, national food crisis intensified beyond the comprehension of even the most cynical critics of the civilian regime (see Tables 2.3 and 2.5 above). This food shortage led to several riots in many urban centres, and coupled with the acrimonies surrounding the elections of 1983, the military intervened again in the political process. The first action taken by the new military government, led by General Buhari, was to abandon the Green Revolution, and thereafter, ordering leading politicians behind the various rural development programmes to be arrested and prosecuted. The military then decided to pursue vigorously the World Bank's funded Agricultural Development Projects (ADPs), two of which I have selected for this study.

In the following chapters, the description and findings of the two villages selected for this study are presented. Both villages have implemented the World Bank's agricultural experiment which specifically aimed at resolving the crisis of agrarian transformation in Nigeria. A third village was also studied, and used as a control village. The control village has not yet implemented the ADPs as in the two villages of our study.

4 The World Bank and Agricultural Development Projects in Southeast Nigeria

Introduction: The Project Area

The World Bank's funded agricultural development programme in Rivers State covers a total land area of 2,800 square kilometres. It stretches from the former Ikwerre and Etche divisions to some parts of Ahoada, Obio and Ogba divisions. An estimated 240,000 peasant farmers reside in this area. Climatic conditions in the project area vary from region to region. On the average, the entire project area is characterized by a long rainy season which begins in March and lasts through the month of November. The majority of peasant farmers in this area derive 70-80 percent of their income from subsistence agriculture which is seasonal. During the off season period, massive migration to coastal areas where fish farming opportunities exist, is widespread.

Land tenure is vested in the clan. In pre-colonial times, decisions regarding allocation of arable land to peasants' families were collectively made by members of the clan. However, this practice of collective decision making was changed with the introduction of the system of warrant chiefs by the British colonial administrators (Afigbo, 1972). At the present time, the clan chief in consultation with the council of elders, is responsible for land allocation to each household under the condition that such land cannot be exchanged or sold for monetary purposes. Usually, the sale of a communal land for family farming could result either in expulsion from the clan or monetery fine.

On the average, a typical peasant household has just about 0.7 hectare of arable land under cultivation. The main staple crop is cassava which is grown primarily for household consumption. Surplus food produce is generally sold or bartered to peasants in riverine areas where farming is hampered by bad terrain. The primary buyers of cassava, and other food items are the riverine Igbos, and the IJaw people of Okrika, Bonny and Eleme. These people specialize in fish farming, and normally trade their catches for agricultural produce.

During colonial times, export related commercial farming was encouraged. The area was famous for producing palm kernel, palm oil, raffia palm, and rubber which were exported to European metropolis. The city of Port Harcourt, which was then the only metropolitan port, served as the centre of commerce between European produce buyers and peasants from the hinterland. Prior to this, the city was also the main slave port in southeastern Nigeria during the slave trade. Increasingly, the city of Port Harcourt is becoming more modernized as most crude petroleum conglomerates have their headquarters there. The population of Port Harcourt metropolis is over a million people most of whom are engaged in trading, farming, and irregular employment with the crude petroleum corporations.

The farming population in the project area consists of Igbo speaking peasants who had migrated to the area prior to the civil war of 1967-70. The migration had been forced upon them by scarcity of land in the Igbo mainland. However, a sizable proportion of those who migrated to the area did so to take advantage of the commercial opportunities offered by the city of Port Harcourt. Ethnic problems between mainland Igbos, who migrated to the area, and the natives continue to undermine good relationships in the area, especially in Ikwerre, in spite of linguistic similarities. The civil war actually intensified traditional hostilities that existed before the war as many migrants Igbos to the area saw their property confiscated during the war period.

Social Structure of the Ikwerre Igbos

Prior to British colonialism, social structure of Ikwerre Igbos was fairly homogeneous with very little stratification (Anikpo, 1985; Dike, 1953). There was hardly any centrally constituted political authority as in most parts of Nigeria. Participatory democracy was the norm (Afigbo, 1972). By 1914, after the British had established full military and political control over the major protectorates of the North, South East and Lagos, the amalgamation decree produced what is now known as Nigeria. Unlike their Hausa-Fulani neighbours to the North, and the Yoruba to the West, the Igbos resisted the British experiment of indirect rule; a political arrangement that the British designed using native elites to rule on behalf of the imperial state.

As it turned out, the indirect rule worked so well among the Hausa-Fulanis because of the existing system of Islamic feudalism which embodies the absolute power of the Emirs, and the provincial caliphates. In the South West, the British also exploited the centralized power of the Yoruba Kings (Oba) to enforce the system of indirect rule. It was the absence of this sort of centralized social hierarchy among the Igbos that led to the establishment of the warrant chiefs. Those targeted by the British for warrant chieftaincy were successful noted Igbo traders, some of whom had openly supported British rule as the only means of securing their commercial advantages as middlemen (Dike, 1953; Afigbo, 1972).

As the political authority of the warrant chiefs became legitimized over time, households' power relations also began to undergo significant changes. In particular, patriarchy became an important force. For example, households previously headed by women became transformed with older men taking over important decisions affecting the household. Similarly, women participation in household production was marginalized to subsistence farming with men dominating commercial farming and long distance trading. Social negotiations over land which were previously determined by age and clan affiliation irrespective of gender, now fell under the exclusive control of older male members of the clan. Thus, the Igbo democratic way of life soon gave way to a feudalistic sort of control only mediated through the older members of the clan (Anikpo, 1985).

The warrant chiefs, in particular, served both the political and economic interests of the British colonialists by providing some kind of artificial institution that allowed for colonial officials to brutally destroy existing patterns of authority and political power formally exercised by the clan elders. The authority of the warrant chiefs could only be enforced through a formidable military backing by the colonial administrators who were bent on supplanting the egalitarian system of rights and obligations that characterized most Igbo precolonial society. Resistance to indirect rule was severely repressed with rebellious clansmen and women given long sentences in the colonial penal system. Older clan members with popular support were routinely uprooted from their villages. The success of the British in supplanting the democratic system of the Igbos was soon to give way to strong anti-British sentiments that finally culminated in the independence movement championed by Dr. Nnamidi Azikiwe and others. In fact, the Aba riots, and the Enugu coalminers' strike in the forties were both the products of the generalized resentments against British rule in Igoland.

Section I: Project Village 1: Ubima Village

Agricultural Development Projects in Rivers State

The first set of World Bank funded agricultural development projects in Nigeria went back to 1971 when the bank provided U.S. $7.2 million for cocoa development projects in the former Western Region. In 1974, the programme was extended to the northern part of the country when it provided loans for the execution of similar projects in Gusua, and Gombe (World Bank document No. 1525-UNI, 1978). It was not until 1975 that the Rivers State government approached the Bank, through the Federal government, for a similar agricultural development loan.

The bank's projects in Rivers State focused on the development of palm oil production in the state. It was later extended to the development of subsidiary export crops such as palm kernel, raffia palm, date palm, and coconut. During colonial times, the region became a prime colonial target because of its abundant oil palm trade, and the easy accessibility to the Atlantic ocean (Dike, 1958). The United African Company (UAC), and Levers Brothers of London, dominated most of the palm trade in southern Nigeria. Palm oil was important for the burgeoning European industrial economy since the oil was processed into margarine and candles in addition to being used in the heavy engineering sector of the metropolitan economy.

But the expansion and further development of oil palm plantations were cut short by the mounting nationalist movement of the late forties shortly after World War II. This led to a shift in colonial interest in oil palm development, as a result of which export crop development was abruptly stopped. The few plantations that were established in eastern Nigeria were either abandoned or sold off to local African traders. At the peak of commercial rubber and oil palm production, European planters and traders relied on smallholding farmers for the production of both crops. With the attainment of independence in 1960, the oil palm based economy of the riverine areas, and other parts in south eastern Nigeria was at the point of collapse. This was partly due to a massive displacement of peasants from the area during the war.

Thus, it was not unexpected that the Rivers State was among the first states in Nigeria to directly seek World Bank funding for the rehabilitation of its oil palm production. Before the bank assistance was sought, the development of good quality oil palm was initially concentrated in the hands of a state owned company named "River State Oil Palm Corporation" (RISONPALM), whose charter includes the overseeing of export crops development in the state, and the supervision of peasants' agricultural production in the project area. As a state agency, RISONPALM became the primary instrument of linking post-war peasants' production to the world market.

RISONPALM: Background Information

In 1974, the Rivers State government set up RISONPALM Ltd as a public limited liability company to coordinate and supervise the palm oil rehabilitation efforts of the government. According to the company's documents and government's white papers, the company was charged with "the responsibility for the development of new varieties of oil palm, and the processing of palm oil, palm kernel and other associated products." (Brief on Risonpalm Limited, 1991:1-2). According to the company's document, the project will involve the development of 10,000 hectares of Oil Palm Nucleus Estate at Elele-Ahoada area, and a 10,000 hectare smallholding in the same area. The Nucleus Estate, according to the World Bank, will be run by RISONPALM, while the smallholding estates will be run by a Smallholder Management Unit (SMU) to be established within the Rivers State Ministry of Agriculture and Natural Resources (document #1525-UNI).

In 1975, RISONPALM was formally incorporated as a state owned enterprise with an authorized share capital of 200,000 shares. By 1983 the company's share capital had increased to 4.40 million. In 1986 the authorized share capital rose to 30 million, and by the time this fieldwork was carried out in 1990, the authorized share capital had grown to 100 million (company documents). This dramatic rise in the company's shares reflected the degree of interest the state government placed on the company as an agent of rapid transformation of the rural economy.

According to the general manager, the company was engaged in negotiating a new loan with the European Economic Commission (EEC), under the Lome II convention, for the development of the lowland region of the State. The company was supposed to be privatized by the mid-1990s in line with the new loan negotiation terms with the EEC. The privatization was one of the central guidelines demanded by the World Bank for the re-structuring of the economy, and failure to adhere to the privatization directive could lead to the freezing of funding.

Prior to the enactment of the military decree that formally incorporated the company in 1975, the Rivers State government commissioned a feasibility study which was carried out by a Belgian consultancy firm - SOCFINCO Ltd. The firm was asked to prepare a feasibility study for the establishment of a commercially viable oil palm estate in the state. The Belgian company produced a report that supported the Rivers State government's position, that the only way to rehabilitate oil palm production in the state to its pre-war level was through the establishment of large estates to be run along capitalist relations of production. In the report, the Belgium firm had projected oil palm production into 1990, when it expected the nucleus estate, and the smallholder project to produce annually 47,000 metric tons of oil palm "for domestic consumption, and 10,126 metric tons of palm kornels for export" (World Bank report, 1978; p.iii). In addition, the report envisaged that at full maturity, the project as a whole would provide salaried and wage employment for 2,000 villagers, and about 35,000 family members would benefit directly or indirectly from the project (bank's document No. 1525-UNI 1978: iii).

Armed with this feasibility study, the Rivers State government approached the World Bank for a $30 million loan which was guaranteed by the Federal Government of Nigeria. The loan represented the largest World Bank's lending to the Nigerian state for the purposes of agricultural development. The loan for the project was granted only with two conditions namely: 1) that alongside the establishment of a large oil palm estate, the company would also earmark part of the money for the development of smallholding farms which would be run and managed by peasant farmers; and 2) that SOCFINCO, the Belgian firm that carried out the feasibility study, be retained to provide technical and managerial services to the projects. In effect, the project was from its inception controlled by foreign experts appointed by the World Bank.

The execution of the project was divided into two phases. The first phase was the development of the Nucleus Estate which was located at the village of Ubima. The second phase was the development of the secondary estates (mini-estates) which were to be managed by peasant farmers in Elele-Ahoada area. The concentration of the smallholder units was at Elele, a few kilometres from the commercial city of Port Harcourt. The two projects, the Nucleus Estate at Ubima and the smallholder project, were surveyed for this study. The villages of Elele and Ubima were centres of oil palm production in the former eastern region during the colonial era. The two villages were briefly disrupted during the civil war as a result of their location on the boundary between the former Biafra nation, and the area controlled by the Nigerian federal troops. The war contributed to the disruption of peasants' production throughout the duration of the civil war which halted oil palm production.

Data 1: Nucleus Estate at Ubima

Ubima is an Ikwerre village a few kilometres from the heartland of Igboland. The community with a population of 16,500 people was destroyed during the civil war that lasted from 1967-70. During the war, the community was annexed as part of the Biafran nation because the majority of the people speak traditional Igbo language even though they claimed different ancestry from the Baifran Igbos. The community is important because it is the main link to the ancient port of Port Harcourt, the only outlet to the sea for the new Biafran nation. The battle to retake Ubima from the Biafran forces by the federal troops left the community almost in ruins. For the duration of the civil war, peasant agricultural production was completely disrupted. The main commercial crops in the area, palm oil and palm kernel, were abandoned by peasant farmers who fled the area for safer havens in the Ibo heartland, and Okrika village on the foot of the Delta. It was not surprising that the area became a target for agricultural revitalization after the war.

Initially, RISONPALM focused on the development of the nucleus estate at Ubima. According to government and RISONPALM documents, 3,500 hectares of peasants' land were acquired without adequate compensation. This was in addition to 4,524 hectares of peasants' land which it inherited from the defunct Eastern Nigeria Development Corporation (ENDC). The company also inherited a total of 1,400 hectares of old varieties of planted oil palm from ENDC. Altogether, the Nucleus Estate at Ubima currently has 10,000 hectares of fully planted oil palm of new and improved varieties.

The estate was managed from 1975-85 by expatriate personnel brought from various European countries by the Belgian consultancy company, SOCFINCO who produced the feasibility study for RISONPALM. From the $30 million loan from the World Bank, the company bought an oil mill that has the capacity of processing 40 tons of fresh fruit bunches per hour (40 ffb/hr). According to company officials, the oil mill is the largest oil processing mill in the whole of Africa. The overriding priority of the Belgian firm, at the initial stages of the establishment of the Nucleus Estate, according to one informant, seemed to have been the comfort and welfare of its expatriate workers. According to

56

company's documents, and also interview excerpts with the company's management, a sizable portion of the loan went into the construction of a satellite village within the project site providing recreation facilities, and internally generated electricity for the comfort and convenience of the foreign experts, and their Nigerian counterparts. Indeed, the feasibility study prepared by the Belgian company, and approved by the World Bank, had recommended that of the $30 million loan, nearly a third of it (U.S. $9.2 million) be set aside for the construction of houses and recreational facilities for the project's management staff, who are predominantly recruited from abroad (bank document No. 1525-UNI, 1978: ii).

The satellite village was also equipped with a bank, amusement park, schools, clean water facilities such as, hydro-pumps, mono-pumps, and bore holes. The most modern of satellite television receivers, that would enable the foreign workers, and the Nigerian senior managers to receive overseas television and cable stations from abroad, were also installed. It is important to note that the peasant villages where these projects are located could hardly boast of any of these facilities even at the time of this survey. The general manager for agronomy and technical services justified the initial expenses, during my interview with him, as the only way the company could draw and retain qualified manpower to the estate.

Land Acquisition and State Intervention

The initial tension between RISONPALM and the peasant community at Ubima was over the question of land acquisition. In Ubima, land ownership and use have been guided for centuries by tradition and customs handed down from generation to generation. In the clan system that characterized the social formation of the Igbo people of Ubima, the clan elder (oldest male member of the clan) is the highest traditional authority wielding political and social power over its subjects.

The clan system is made up of several villages, each united by claim to a common origin and linguistic similarities. The clan chief's authority was, however, the making of the British colonialists. Before British colonialism, the Igbo society and institutions were democratic and acephalous (Anikpo, 1984; Afigbo, 1972). As was mentioned earlier on, the British introduced the system of warrant chiefs at the turn of the century to facilitate British rule, and to simplify the system of tax collection (hut tax) imposed on the natives by the British colonialists. The chief, who today is both the political leader of the clan, and the link to tradition, exercises considerable power over land allocation and use. By traditional norm, no individual member of the clan could sell communal land that is allocated to him or her by the chief.

Since the introduction of the system of warrant chieftaincy, land is allocated to each extended family by the clan chief. The head of the family then allocates land to able bodied members of each household. By Igbo custom, women are excluded from land allocation except for single women who by tradition could not marry out of the clan, or widowers who lost their husbands, and who could not return to their own family because of the elaborate system of bride price (Badru, 1987). However, women could be allowed the use of a plot of land allocated to their husbands in so far as such plots are used only for subsistence farming. In theory, the use of family plot is the personal property of the household but once it is not put into proper use, any member of the clan could claim it. However, with widespread commodity production, and the introduction and expansion of the ADPs, land sale is becoming an acceptable social and economic practice among the Ikwerre people. The exception is that no communal land could be exchanged for monetary value. Increasingly, family plots are now becoming personal assets of individuals or families who put such land into use. Land left fallow for a number of years automatically becomes part of the communal land and could be distributed in any matter the clan elder wishes. However, such land cannot be taken over by the clan chief. The clan chief must exercise prudence in the ways he allocates land otherwise his authority will be subject to questioning.

When the state government attempted to acquire land from the Ubima community in early 1975 for the agricultural projects (ADPs), the community resisted, thus delaying the plans on the establishment of the Nucleus Estate. However by 1976, the federal military government was forced by pressure from oil multinational corporations and projects' officials to enact a decree (Land Use Act of 1978) which appropriated land nationally from traditional rulers, and making peasants' land the property of the state (Turner and Badru, 1984:7). This decree allowed the state government to acquire land from the community for the establishment of the oil palm estate. As this author discovered, those who lost land to the project were poor peasants, and women in the two categories outlined above. During the data collection phase of this research, the villagers pointed out to this research team that the only way the government could enforce the 1978 Land Use Decree, alienating peasants' land, was by colluding with the clan chiefs, and titled peasants (lower rank warrant chiefs), whom they believed had been bought off by the promise of government contracts once the project was firmly

58

established. Thus, it was not surprising that resistance to land alienation, and demand for better compensation for land acquired so far, continued to come from women's organizations and younger men, whose livelihood, and economic independence were being undermined and threatened by the projects (Turner, 1991).

This opposition to land acquisition has often been brutally repressed by the state. For instance, there was the recent case of the Umuechem village in Rivers States, a few kilometres away from Ubima, involving a confrontation between peasants and Texaco Oil International corporation which had acquired peasants' land for oil exploitation (crude petroleum). When the peasants, whose land had been acquired, blockaded the entrance to the premises of the oil company, anti-riot police were dispatched to retake the premises. At the end of the stand-off, several villagers were killed, including the chief of the village (Guardian Newspaper, March 22, 1992, p.11; CLO report 1990, p.11). This type of incident, according to the villagers, was a common occurrence, and the Nigerian state always sided with the oil corporations even when the peasants' claim against the oil multinationals was a legitimate one.

Capitalist Agriculture vs. Peasant Production

The Nucleus Estate at Ubima is run on an elaborate dual system of labour organization. It combines a capitalist relation of production with a petty commodity form of production. The main estate is run on a capitalist wage system while the mini-estates are organized around a mixture of petty commodity production, and a share cropping system that is rather too complex. However, the best way to understand this complex system of labour organization at the Ubima Nucleus Estate is through the analysis of social stratification that is specific to this peasant community. This analysis will focus on the disruption in preexisting social formation including the system of reward status and communal cooperation which are now being increasingly destroyed by the ADPs.

Social Structure of Ubima Village

The peasantry at the project site is stratified based on the traditional system of ranking introduced by the British. The stratification is based primarily on status, and also on the relationship of each individual peasant to the means of production, which in this case, is land. On the one hand, we have a social group defined by the chiefly status without direct regards to their position within the system of production. On the other hand, we have the absentee farmers who by their dominant social and economic position have access to disproportionate amount of communal land made possible by the land use decree. This group of peasants also has easy access to credit, capital and modern technology. They also have the financial capability of employing other peasants and seasonal workers as wage labourers. In the case of the former category of farmers, entry into the chiefly class is based on tradition and heredity. The exception to this is the case of the newly rich urban based absentee farmers whose social status as a chief is purely honorary, and in recognition of their newly found wealth. In Igboland, those who left the village for the city in search of a better life routinely returned to the village to seek social status which they previously lacked. These two groups exert considerable influence on the project administration. Below the chiefly class, and the absentee farmers, are clusters of peasants in five categories which we discuss below.

At the next step of the stratification ladder, we have the upper or rich peasants, the middle peasantry, the lower middle peasantry, the poor or lower peasantry, and the bonded peasantry, other wise known as the outcast (osu). The distinction made here was based on three criteria namely; a) wealth in land, and head count of live animals especially goats; b) credit ratings based on the amount of farm currently farmed, and type of technology deployed; c) ability to hire other peasant farmers (non-reliance on family labour). As it turned out, the rich farmers control between 10-15 hectares of land, and they constitute two percent of the peasant population. They employed, on average, 25 peasants working regularly on their farm.

The middle peasantry has under cultivation between 5-10 hectares of land, and they also employ on average, 10 permanent farm labourers. In addition to employing their family members as labourers, the lower middle peasantry also relies on seasonal or migrant labourers especially during the high season. On average, the middle peasants have up to 5 hectares of land under cultivation. The lower, and the poor peasants cultivate somewhere between a third of a hectare to 1.5 hectares of land. The only distinction between the poor peasant, and the lower peasantry is that the poor peasants spend a significant part of the year working on the farms of the rich peasants, or sometimes migrating to the lowland areas where fishing opportunities are available during the off season. The majority of the lower peasantry in my sample also work as messengers and janitors in the government civil service as a way of supplimenting their meagre income. They usually only return to their farm after office hours.

The bonded peasants or outcasts (osu) are something peculiar to this area. They are on the margin of being social outcasts and indentured labourers. They have come to the area because of scarcity of land in their own clan. These are the categories of rural peasants that European scholars often identified as slaves. In actual fact, these are individuals whose stay in the clan is temporary. The class of "osu" is made up of young men who have bonded themselves out in order to raise money for bride price. This group could remain in bondage for a period of seven years. We found that the rural development projects sited in these peasant's communities, as I discuss later, have also contributed to the rise in the numbers of young men who doubled both as bonded peasants and seasonal workers on the main plantation.

These outcast peasants have no rights to land whatsoever. They can only lay claim to the crops they plant through the male head of the peasant household to whom they are bonded. Indeed, during an earlier study (Badru, 1985), this category of peasants were found to be those who stood to lose everything during land acquisition either by the World Bank or oil multinationals. The reason being that money paid on damaged crops during oil exploration were usually paid directly to the person who holds title to the land, and not to those bonded peasants who actually planted the crops.

There is some interesting gender based stratification in the project villages. In the villages surveyed for this study, nearly a third of the middle peasantry are women, who by their traditional status, cannot marry (first daughter of a chief), or widows who remain within the clan because they cannot afford to repay the bride wealth paid to their clan by their husbands. This category of peasant women employ male labourers from the ranks of the bonded peasants, and their farms are usually supervised by a male relative or a concubine. In short, this increasing stratification among the peasantry may account for the failure of this community to effectively organize against land acquisition either by the project authority or by foreign oil multinationals. Indeed, the main conflict as we observed was often between the chiefly class, especially the rich and influential segment of the class, and the young men and women who made up the lower rank of the lower peasantry.

In fact, of the 6,000 wage labourers at the Ubima Nucleus Estate, 80 percent are men and women from the category of lower peasantry while the remaining 20 percent are migrant labourers from upland Igboland. Of the total wage labourers at the Nucleus Estate, women constitute 65 percent. It is important to note that the main estate draws its labour force from the entire geographical spread of the state in an effort to satisfy the ethnic quota requirements of the state government, and these are usually enforced by the projects' adminstrators.

Section II: The Main Estate: Organizational Structure

At its inception in 1978, the Ubima Nucleus Estate was run by SOCFINCO Consultants International, and RISONPALM, the Rivers State's agency responsible for integrated rural development at the time. Overall, there are three divisions at the estate namely; Technical Support Division, Management Division, and Marketing and Extension Services Division. The management division coordinates the other divisions and is headed by a project manager or general manager. The general manager is assisted by three assistant managers who are respectively in charge of the three other main units. The assistant managers oversee the day today operation, supervision of the field officers who are in regular contact with peasant farmers participating in the programme.

RISONPALM employs a total of 6,000 workers, 60 percent of whom work directly on the fields or on the processing assembly complex. The estate is highly capitalized, and the work process is somewhat regimental. The organization of work, and work ethics at the main estate are very different from what the peasant farmers are accustomed to. The management staff is made up of the remaining 40 percent. The majority of these are extension workers who work directly with the peasant farmers on experimental farms. Many of them have been redeployed from the state Ministry of Agriculture and Rural Development.

At the main Nucleus Estate, the most modern agricultural equipments were deployed making it one of the most mechanized plantations in sub-Saharan Africa. The machinery used included combine harvesters, tractors, and a 40 ton fruit bunches per hour (40 ffb/hr) oil processing mill. Most of the equipments were supplied by Caterpillar International, and Peugeot, a French auto-maker. The money for procuring the equipments came from the first instalment of the World Bank loan. The management refused to tell this research team how much these equipments cost or the means of their procurement. The only thing we gathered was that the equipments were procured by SOCFINCO, the Belgian company retained by the World Bank to manage the project (Interview excerpts with RISONPALM managers). In the early stages of the programme, financial management and high level decision making were left for the SOCFINCO senior officers without having to share crucial information with their Nigerian counterparts. This was actually a key provision of the loan agreement designating total execution and management of the programme to the foreign contract agency. The underlining assumption is that local managers could not perform as well as those imported from abroad. But the problem here is that by importing local managers, projects' expenses tended to go up compared to using local personnel whose salaries are much lower than their expatriate counterparts. Besides, there is no evidence to suggest that expatriate personnel are better qualified than locally trained ones.

Emoluments

The workers on the main estate are normally offered two types of emoluments. Workers can either choose an hourly rate that pays something between five to six naira per hour (roughly U.S. 20 cents), or they can choose to work on a piece rate that pays 13 naira per piece. This dual system of reward, as we discovered, has created hostility between workers who remained on hourly rate, and those on piece rates. The decision to stay on either one depends on the specific function performed by the worker. Those who are in the more physically demanding functions such as climbing palm trees, felling old plantings, and fruits picking are encouraged by the management to stay on piece rate contract which is relatively lucrative. Those who trim palm trees, and assembly line workers, the majority of whom are women, tended to stay on the hourly wage system.

The system was designed, according to one union member, to forestall any possible organization against the management. But management denied this. The management claimed that the dual pay system was introduced to encourage competition, and to draw the most able workers to the more demanding, and remunerative jobs. However, management agreed that women were barred from certain jobs because of their hazardous nature.

Benefits and Conditions at the Main Estate

Benefits and work conditions at the estate are rather too poor. Except for the junior worker's health clinic which attends to nearly 600 patients a week, the majority of the employees enjoy few benefits. This is contrary to what the general manager claimed during an interview session. In fact, the majority of the workers still travel the 40 kilometre journey to the main teaching hospital in Port Harcourt. This contrasts sharply with the facilities at the management quarters where the consultants and the senior Nigerian managers reside.

The work routine on the main estate at Ubima is extremely harsh to peasants. Most of the complaints from the farm labourers we interviewed on the site, centred around the inflexibility of the supervisors whom they said run the estate like a military camp. Those farm labourers housed on the estate camps complained of unsanitary conditions, and harassment from camp security personnel which often results in scuffles between the guards and peasants working on the plantation. This explains why a significant number of wage labourers opted to live in the village, and to walk daily to work without any transportation allowance from the company. This condition is somewhat reminiscent of the conditions of migrant farm workers in South Africa and Mozambique where migratory labour on European plantations is the norm. Because of the relatively low wages paid on the Nucleus Estate, many of the peasant farmers return to their personal plots after the gruelling twelve hours day work on the field to compliment their earnings. Heads of registered households usually send their wives and unmarried daughters to the estate for paid employment during the off season period. As a result of this seasonal employment, most of the women in our sample are most like to resent male authority pattern which is most visible on the plantations and in individual households. This resentment stems from the double burden of women working as wage labourers, and as main reproducers of the peasant's households. The reason behind this double exploitation may be found in the rigid division of labour within the household which is still enforced in spite of the fact that many peasant women are increasingly drawn into the wage sector by the economic necessity imposed by land acquisition.

Success at the Expense of Whom?

Whatever progress this project has brought to this village is very hard to determine. The general manager claimed that the project performance to date is an unqualified success. Evaluation reports commissioned by the company and by the World Bank painted an encouraging picture of how the pilot projects have transformed the peasant community. However, these reports often used as their terms of reference, economic indices while ignoring vital social indicators that are pertinent to an overall assessment of the projects' successes or failures. However, the most visible success story may be said to be the expanding capacity of the Nucleus Estate, and the increased productivity on the main oil palm plantation.

Since SOCFINCO left in 1983, records shown to us revealed that RISONPALM has been able to revitalize palm oil production to its pre-independence level. The company no longer relies on the state government to pay its operating cost, and according to the assistant general manager, the company has been able to generate resources internally to embark on its diversification programme. Company documents made available to this research team showed a production capacity of 719,554 metric tons of fresh fruit bunches over a period of less than ten years. These were processed into 102,179 metric tons of special palm oil for export. This contrasted favourably to the less than 5,000 metric tons annual production before the estate was taken over by RISONPALM under the rural integrated development programme (RISONPALM Newsletters, 1986-92). In addition, about 34,221 metric tons of palm kernel at an average extraction rate of between 14 and 28 per cent for special palm oil (spo), and 4 percent for palm kernel were produced. In fact, the five year production output of 719,554.90 metric tons, representing an annual output of 143,910.98 metric tons, was far greater than the World Bank's projected estimate of 47,250 metric tons "when the project reached maturity in 1990" (World Bank document No. 15225-UNI, 1978: iii).

All of these have been achieved as a result of the drastic re-organization of the labour process, and the introduction of the principles of scientific management. This scientific management practice often conflicts with peasants' traditional attitude to nature and work, and it is clearly out of touch with peasants' social realities. The profound clash between this new scientific production ethos and the sort of changes in social relations that these entail will be discussed in the next chapter. In the current 1990-95 production plan, the company's diversification strategies put emphasis on the production of new varieties of quality palm kernel and palm kernel cake of which 1,615.41 metric tons have been produced to date. The new diversification will also involve the production of technical palm oil (tpo), palm kernel shells, and empty bunches. How much this development on the Nucleus Estate has helped the peasant economy on which it is located is very difficult to pinpoint.

Perhaps differences of opinion between the management and the peasant farmers, whose lives have been transformed by the experiment, is understandable. During discussion sessions with RISONPALM management and World Bank officials at the ADPs headquarters in Port Harcourt, the impression this researcher got was that there was a fundamental, if not contradictory view of what the whole project represents to the community. Visits to Ubima community itself, and talking with community leaders, teachers, and local politicians revealed a deep seated antagonism between the agents of change, in this case the project administrators, and the target population, the peasant farmers. Nearly everyone we talked to in the village denied the claim by RISONPALM that the company has come through on its promises to provide amenities for the community. At the main estate, senior company officials, and block supervisors told this researcher that RISONPALM has provided mono-pumps, electricity, etc. In particular, the villagers denied the claim by the company that it has provided scholarships for children of school age to the tune of five million naira over the past years. The villagers saw these claims by RISONPALM as a propaganda exercise. Such propaganda, we were told, were often used as guises to acquisition more peasants' land.

When this author tried to corroborate the company's claims, he was given a list of company's contact persons. These individuals turned out to be discredited chiefs who collaborated with the Belgian company, SOCFINCO, and the project's administrators during the initial phase of land acquisition. The people we were directed to by the project's management tended to confirm the company's story line. Independent informants (generally peasants and local intellectuals at the University of Port Harcourt) painted a different picture.

The discrepancies between peasants and management's assessment of the project revealed deep seated antagonisms. For instance, the general manager refused to acknowledge the fact that the pilot estate has generated considerable antagonisms and structural changes within the community. When asked to comment on the social impact of land acquisition, especially the exclusion of women from registering as a potential head of household in the company's supervised collectivization programme, the manager dismissed the discussion as irrelevant. However, in a newspaper interview which the project manager gave a week after we visited the Nucleus Estate, he acknowledged the question of forced land acquisition from the community as the most serious issue that continues to cloud the company's credibility at the village level, and more so, its claim to success in the community.

The manager acknowledged in the interview thus:

> Land acquisition is vital to oil palm industry. A lot of enlightenment is
> required to persuade the people to offer their land for development and

cultivation. It is hoped that the social amenities that go with Risonpalm operation, the people will be willing to give out their land (Concord newspaper, March 12, 1992, p.14).

Generally, peasants negative reaction to the project centres around the break down of direct communication between the higher echelon of RISONPALM who are likely to delegate authority and supervision to extension workers. Indeed, the newly found social status of the extension workers has placed them in a direct opposition to the chiefs whose support for the projects may determine its failure or success. Besides these antagonistic relations between the extension workers and the chiefs, the villagers also accused the extension workers of corruption and duplicity in the manner in which they discharged their duties.

For example, provision of technical assistance and marketing facilities to smallholder peasants is the most divisive issue in the project's sites. Extension workers routinely deny extension services to those peasants they labelled as "stubborn" and "resistant to change". In fact, as it was discovered during this field research, those peasant farmers labelled "stubborn" were those who had demanded more popular participation in the extension delivery system.

Farm inputs such as fertilizers, medium scale farm implements, gloves, and foot wares were used as means of rewarding peasants who cooperate with the extension officers during their Training and Visiting (T & V) sessions. It became apparent that coercing peasants into either giving their plots into the collectives or turning their plots into experimental farms, are the surest means of forcing them off to the Nucleus Estate's wage employment. This is particularly so with women who manage family plots independent of their husbands or male relatives.

Gender Based Discrimination at the Main Estate

A closer look at the project design revealed that women were excluded from the ranks of peasant farmers targeted for capitalist farming. The majority of the target farmers, the so-called "progressive farmers" are men. Thus, it is no wonder that resistance to this indirect system of enclosure has its most militant expression in the ranks of peasant women, who more than their male counterparts consistently challenged the authority of the project administrator.

For instance, during one of our visits we were invited to a burial ceremony of a female leader who had organized a successful boycott of RISONPALM in 1988 by urging other women to take their fresh fruit bunches to independent millers in the adjourning villages. At the funeral ceremony, women danced to songs that extolled the virtues of cooperative spirit among the villagers, and denounced, in their songs and dances, collaborators with project officials whom they accused of selling fertilizers that were assigned for the collectives.

In all, women are discriminated against by the design of the project which is male focused. Our investigation revealed that women have the roughest deal both in terms of their ability to participate in the independent collectives, and as wage labourers at the main estate. Most women on the plantations work a shift starting at six in the morning, and ending sometime at dawn. The division of labour restricted them to picking fresh fruit bunches or trimming palm trees under the most hazardous conditions. For instance women trimmers were hardly provided with protective clothing, and in most cases, have no protection against inhaling insecticides.

The majority of women who work at the Nucleus Estate were excluded from junior staff housing that was provided for their male counterparts. The average income of women labourers is far below those of men, and in some cases, half of what the men on piece rates make. This is due in part to the company's labour policy that restricted performance of certain jobs for male labourers. For instance, women were excluded from piece rate jobs where they could earn 13 naira an hour as opposed to the five naira they make trimming fruit bunches. This division tends to affect solidarity between female and male workers at the estate especially when it comes to organizing around issues that affect all categories of workers at the estate. Generally, management often play one set of workers against the other by encouraging unfair clan rivalry amongst them.

Section III: Mini-Estates: Smallholding Collectives

Alongside the Nucleus Estate at Ubima are mini-estates organized into collectives by RISONPALM management as part of the World Bank's guidelines for smallholding development. The smallholding collectives are directly managed by peasant farmers under the supervision of the extension office. The experimental farms are designed around the modest principle of helping peasants to improve their productivity through the adoption of new techniques, and extension services advice from the Nucleus Estate officers. However, this novel principle seems to have some fundamental flaws. Projects managers at the Nucleus Estate continue to capitalize on the collectives for their own advantage.

According to the project's guideline, each household was asked to donate

2.5 hectares of land into the smallholding experimental farms. Then, 10 of such households were grouped into a farming block. Each block is headed by a contact farmer who works directly with the extension agent. A group of farming blocks is supervised by an extension supervisor. At the time of this study, there were 25 such farming blocks. The hierarchical structure of the collectives allows the company to monitor peasant production closely. In addition, it also enables management, through the extension office staff, to have overall control over their production schedule, and the marketing of their produce.

The company generally provides farm inputs such as technical and extension advice, fertilizers, and medium range farm equipments. In return for the provision of farm inputs, the company has the right to the entire output of these farms. Peasants on the collectives were forbidden from selling their produce to outsiders, and they cannot use nearby independent millers to process their palm kernel. As a result of this rigid arrangement, RISONPALM exerts a monopoly control over the entire marketing, and crop processing system. This overall control forces the peasant farmers in the experimental farms to depend on the company's elaborate system of clientelism. Managers routinely assigned peasants arbitrarily to different functions, and usually those peasants who are more sympathetic to the management style are most likely to be assigned to better paying jobs on the Nucleus Estate.

As it turns out, the marketing division of RISONPALM has exclusive rights to purchase all the produce from the experimental farms at below market price. According to the assistant general manager, the company purchases a fresh fruit bunch for 300 naira per metric ton. But we discovered that farmers could get up to 600 naira per metric ton from independent produce buyers in nearby city centres such as Port Harcourt or Owweri. This marketing arrangement allows the company to doubly exploit the peasants. For example, once the produce is purchased by the company, it proceeds to deduct from the income of the collectives (highest peasants' production unit), cost of providing inputs, and technical advice to the smallholding farmers. The balance, if any at all, is then made available for distribution among the members of the collectives.

According to the members of the collectives, participating members are yet to receive payments from the company since the experimental farms started almost eight years ago. This was due to the fact that all income from the experimental farms have been kept by RISONPALM as capital outlay and repayment of initial credits advanced to the collectivized farms. The majority of those registered in the collectives continue to subsist on income from family plots that were not registered under the programme. Others who were not so fortunate to have family plots to rely on for subsistence took irregular employment from the main Nucleus Estate.

At the main estate, this researcher raised the question of the withholding of collectives' income by RISONPALM's management. We were told that it was part of the original agreement with the peasant farmers before they registered with the programme. In a somewhat illogical reasoning, the general manager justifies this practice thus:

> The problem we had before was that we left the management and technical assistance to the farmers themselves. And because they cannot compromise the long gestation period of the new crop variety supplied to them, they simply abandoned their plots. They switched those plots to food crops production, and other crops that could immediately give them cash. If you give money to farmers they will not use the money for what you gave them for. So, we took over the farms from the smallholding farmers, the production phase; that way, we will be able to recover our initial investment (Interview excerpts, 1992).

This condescending attitude toward the peasants is widespread among the management staff and extension workers. During the series of interviews with members of the management at RISONPALM, and at the Rivers State Rural Development headquarters in Port Harcourt, derogatory remarks about peasants' farming ability were routinely made. These condescending views towards the peasants were often the cause of the numerous conflicts that have plagued the project since its inception. There were reports of peasants chasing extension workers out of their farms in addition to threatening them physically. At one of the field days organized by the block supervisors, we overheard extension workers admonishing peasants for "insubordination" because of, as one of the extension officers insisted, "their refusal to recognize the technical authority of the extension workers" (interviews, 1991).

While it is premature to make any conclusion at this point, it appears as if there are fundamental differences between management and peasant farmers as to the view of how the project should be run. The refusal of extension experts to examine how peasants' knowledge of their environment and their well tested techniques of production could be incorporated into the new scientific technique being introduced may account for some of the frictions and difficulties the project managers are currently facing.

In sum, the rate at which change is being introduced into this farming community has indeed created some doubts in the minds of the peasants as to the real purpose of the project. And given the uncertainty of the future being promised, the peasants' fear may be well founded. There is no doubt that the introduction of the agricultural modernization program into these peasant communities has impacted on their social structure, most especially production relations. The partial co-existence between the old attitudes and the emerging new modern ethos has created a sort of social anomaly which often characterize societies at the edge of change. In the following chapter, we examine the data collected in the second village of Elele. The emphasis of the programme here is on the development of small scale collective mini-estates.

5 Project Village 2: The Elele Mini-Estates

Section I: The Project Area: A Brief Description of the Impact of Crude Petroleum Exploration on Peasants' Agriculture

This second project village is one of the many villages in the project area that have been severely affected by crude oil exploration. Because of its location at the centre of the largest deposit of crude petroleum, the community has struggled to survive the encroaching tenacity of oil multinationals. The Elele community spread over into the Igbo farming areas of Oguta, Obirikom and Izombe. In 1984, a pilot study of these villages by this author revealed the extent of economic devastation which had been brought upon these communities since the start of crude exploration in the early 1970s (Badru, 1984). These villages rely on trade exchange involving food items produced by peasants at Elele, and fish farming by peasants at Oguta, Obirikom and Izombe. Since the intensification of crude exploitation in the area, the economy of these communities have been brought to a virtual standstill. In the following pages we describe the sort of economic misfortunes that have been visited on the villagers by crude oil multinationals. Indeed, the destruction of peasant production by crude exploration made this area a target for the World Bank assisted agricultural projects (ADPs).

Peasants and Big Oil Corporations: The Case of Oguta, Obirikom, Izombe

These three villages are peasant communities that harbour the largest deposit of known crude petroleum in south eastern Nigeria. The Igbos are the most dominant ethnic group in this project area. The three villages survive on petty commodity production. The land, which is the only means of reproduction, is also controlled by the clan whose authority is exercised through the council of elders. Crude oil

72

exploitation was interrupted during the long civil war of 1967-70 that claimed three million lives. Before the outbreak of civil war, oil exploration rights in this area were held by Elf, the French oil multinational. As a result of the war, the French oil workers were forced to flee the area as the federal troops bombarded the area in an attempt to stop oil production for the rebel forces of Biafra. Throughout the duration of the war, the French government continued to give monetary and technical support to the Biafran army in exchange for oil rights once the war was favourably concluded by the Biafran state. However after the war, the rights of exploration promised to the French were cancelled, and the British, American, and Italian oil multinationals moved in to take the place of the French oil multinational. We describe below the experiences of these villages with the oil multinationals.

Obirikom

The Obirikom community is located on the border between the Rivers and the Imo States. The community relies exclusively on smallholding farming. Some peasants supplement their income and diet by engaging in fishing and other assorted activities. Women are particularly involved in farming, and they constitute a greater proportion of the smallholder farmers, specializing in food production. The menfolk engage in cash crops production.

The Obiafu/Obirikom gas injection plant was commissioned in 1985. The project was conceived as a solution to the wastage of gas flaring. The area has however, been subjected to serious ecological dislocation. The siting of this gas injection plant, in the immediate surrounding of this village, has produced a serious physiological effect on the peasant farmers. Some of the villagers we spoke to looked visibly worn out. They all complained of unstoppable sweating and continuous dehydration of the skin caused by the sheer intensity of energy and heat produced by the gas flaring which was just about 200 metres away from the peasants' huts. At the Obirikom/Obiafu gas injection site, we met with six leaders of the peasants whose farms we earlier visited. The interview with the group lasted one-and-a-half hours. During the course of the interview, this researcher was told that since the inception of oil operation in the area, plants and food crops have not been able to bear fruit due to gas flaring. Besides, at least seven peasant's family farms were affected by Agip operation in the area. A total of 61.2 hectares of land was affected.

The peasants' leaders recollected that the land was already surveyed and taken over before the landlords were contacted. According to them, the Federal Government Land Use Decree Act of 1978 rendered the peasants impotent. The decree gave the oil prospecting firms undue upper hand in acquiring peasants' land. By this decree, the oil firm is only obliged to pay compensation to peasants on commercial trees affected by virtue of the oil exploration. No land rent was paid (Badru, 1984).

The land was surveyed in 1980 by Arcies Surveyors (Nigeria) Ltd. At the end of the surveying, 61.2 hectares of land were affected, and Agip, the principal prospecting firm in the area, agreed to pay N60,480.00 in compensation for commercial trees and crops destroyed. In the final stage of negotiation, only N1,000 per acre of land of commercial trees was paid to farmers. Whereas in the adjourning Bendel state, the same Agip paid N4,000 per acre of land. From this information, we enquired from the peasants' leaders how they contacted Agip in the first place. This author was told that a paid agent working for the same oil multinational represented the community. Since the oil multinational appointed one of its own agents to represent the community, it appears the negotiation was a big joke right from the beginning. One member of the group pointed out that the same agent is an established contractor for Agip hence he must have known in advance that the land was to be purchased.

At the end of the negotiation, the agent received a third of the total amount of the compensation paid by the oil company. Some of the peasants, at least a good majority of them, were not very happy with the role played by this agent. They claimed that at the time of the acquisition they were ignorant of the letters of the Land Use Decree. They also claimed that if the acquisitions were to be negotiated now, they would have pressed for the normal rate of land rentals, and perhaps, could have done away with the middleman. The community leaders claimed that at the beginning of oil prospecting, Agip management made a lot of promises. In many cases officials simply make promises to keep the peasants from disrupting crude oil production, and even in cases when Agip comes through on its promise, it is usually a half hearted gesture. Today some of what it has promised to do for the community include:

(a)   provision of free education for their children up to University level;

b)   giving priority to the indigenous at the Agip training;

74

(c)   jobs and contract opportunities for their children and small businesses.

But according to the community leaders interviewed, the company could do better than this given the amount of profit it makes annually from this community. The farmers interviewed also insisted that they were not actually sure of the actual acreage of land acquired by the oil giant for its operation from the area, they only go along with whatever its agent told them during the phase of negotiation. The agents are usually Agip's officials working in the survey and land acquisition department.

Izombe

Izombe consists of nineteen different sub-villages, and oil explorations are in two of the villages - Ugbele and Amaudala. According to the Eze (Chief), oil exploration in the area started in the early sixties with SAFRAP- now Elf as the main oil company. However, the prospecting for oil by SAFRAP came to an end as a result of the civil war. At the end of the war, the Nigerian National Petroleum Corporation (NNPC) revived oil prospecting rights replacing Elf by an American oil corporation, Ashland, as the technical partner.

In Izombe, unlike the Ovbiafu and Obirikom communities, land had already been acquired by the oil company before the promulgation of the 1978 Land Use Decree. At the time, land rental was paid to the Local Government Authority. In the area, Ashland has 25 wells and Gulf only five. Most of the dealings with the oil companies were carried out through the local organization of the village elite called the Izombe Town Development Union (ITDU). The village chief, who is also the president of ITDU, claimed that Ashland has been particularly helpful to the community. A total of eight scholarships are to be awarded yearly by Ashland, while Ashland has also made monetary contribution to the development efforts of the community. According to the Chief, the Land Use Decree of 1978 should be scrapped because he thought the decree was formulated either (a) for government to own oil fields, or (b) to exercise overall control over oil exploration.

On the question of compensation, the oil companies continue to owe the community a total of N4 million (then 4.5 million U.S. dollars) for the destruction of commercial crops and trees. The community leaders claimed that the oil companies only pay for crops within one kilometre of their operation, anything outside the operation is unpaid for. This compares quite favourably with the situation in the Rivers State where the oil companies only pay for crops within 300 metres of their operation.

Turning to the question of ecological and environmental disasters produced by the oil exploration, the Eze (chief) enumerated a number of destructions which oil exploration has caused, and continues to cause, the community over the past ten years. These include among other things, stunted growth of food and commercial crops in the immediate surrounding of flow stations and gas flaring area. The chief implied that since oil exploration began, there have been frequent cases of premature births and deformities of all kinds in new born babies. According to the village head, 250 cases of abortion have been reported to date, and the fear in the community was that this type of crude oil related abortions are most likely to rise.

Oguta

The oil fields at Oguta in this author's judgment provided the most interesting information. This was partly due to the cooperation of our knowledgeable informant who is also a landlord. The Oguta oil field is dominated by Shell Oil Company and Agip. Between them, they operate 74 wells and lift 50,000 barrels of oil daily. Shell alone has 48 oil wells. The Oguta community suffered tremendously from Shell's operations and from village accounting records, made available to the research team, Shell has refused to keep to any safety procedures around its operation. This refusal has exposed peasant farmers to serious hazards unmatched by any location previously visited at Izombe, Ebocha or indeed, Obirikom.

According to the informant, Shell's management has adopted a policy of "not giving-in to the villagers' demand". Apart from market stalls, to which the company contributed some money toward erection, Shell company has virtually ignored the social amenities demanded by the people. In all the farms visited, this researcher noticed cases of stunted crops and widespread destruction caused by beetles and insects. The beetles are continuously attracted to peasants' plots by the illumination from the gas flaring. The beetles caused enormous damage to root crops, especially yam tubers and cassavas. They also invade the huts of the peasants at night. Apart from the farms, fish ponds have also been blocked by oil operations making fish farming in the area a thing of the past. Several burrow pits were left uncared for. In one of such burrow pits villagers drew water for drinking. The villagers made several representations to Shell management to have a portable water device installed at the centre of the village, but to no avail.

In the following section, we discuss the survey of the Elele community whose agricultural production has been obviously affected by crude exploration. The project here, unlike Ubima, is based on small estates cooperatively owned by peasant smallholder farmers receiving technical advice from the ADP directorate.

Section II: The Smallholder Project

The destruction of peasants' livelihood, most especially the dislocation of their farms by crude oil exploration, necessitated the mini-estates project which we have chosen for our second study. The Elele project is also funded by the World Bank. However, the guiding principle and organizational emphasis are slightly different from the Nucleus Estate at Ubima. The focus here is more on the development of smallholders' mini-estates that will be run and controlled entirely by peasant producers themselves. This smallholder project is important for this study because it is one of the oldest integrated rural agricultural modernization programme before the break up of the Nigerian regional structure in 1967 shortly before the outbreak of the civil war. It became part of the World Bank assisted programme in 1978. Up until 1987, it was directly supervised by RISONPALM in line with the World Bank's loan condition. However before we discuss the data collected here, it is important to discuss the general principle and the organizational structure of the agency that is responsible for the supervision of integrated rural development projects in the state. This agency is called Rivers State Agricultural Development Project (RISADEP). The agency was established in 1987 by the state government with considerable assistance from the World Bank. It now supervises a state wide agricultural development programme with direct funding from the World Bank and the federal government of Nigeria. The state government provides infrastructure and logistical support for the projects that fall under the jurisdiction of RISADEP. Its operation was placed directly under the jurisdiction of the state ministry of agriculture whose commissioner exercised tremendous power on the location of the project state-wide.

RISADEP Organization and Management Structure

In early 1987, the state government decided to embark on a state-wide integrated rural development programme. Nearly ten years after the establishment of the

Nucleus Estate at Ubima, the state government announced the establishment of Rivers State Agricultural Development Project as an organ for rural development (RISADEP). According to the agency's newsletter the organization's primary objectives include among other things:

a) To increase production and income of smallholder farmers and fishermen, and to improve the living standard of rural population;

b) Help streamline extension services and the input delivery system;

c) To improve the network of rural roads;

d) To make available, at least in a small way, safe portable water to the rural population (Newsletter, Vol.1, no.1, 1987).

In other to achieve these objectives, the agency relies on an elaborate organizational structure that is very bureaucratic and with emphasis on technocratic competence.

Organizationally, RISADEP is highly centralized. At the top is the ADP Executive Committee (ADPEC); a committee that wields absolute power over the administration of smallholder projects throughout the state. The executive committee formulates and executes all policies affecting the smallholding farmers without prior consultation with the people at the village level. The committee is made up of fourteen members most of whom are state commissioners and local assembly deputies. The project manager serves as secretary to the committee. Below the ADPEC is a Project Management Unit (PMU) which sometimes initiates and implements policies on behalf of the executive committee for the ADP. The project manager heads the PMU. He singlehandedly decides on production schedules, production quotas and admission of new peasants into the smallholding projects. The project manager also decides on which stratum of the peasantry qualifies to receive the agency's technical assistance and farm inputs.

In theory, the PMU is subordinate to the ADPEC, but in practice it often operates independent of the executive committee. The Project Management Unit (PMU) convenes a Monthly Technical Review Meeting (MTRM) which is attended by the project staff and resource persons who essentially are specialists in their different disciplines. The resource persons are drawn periodically and randomly from various research institutes from all over the country. Most of these resource persons work for the World Bank funded Tropical Agricultural Institute at Ibadan, western Nigeria.

At the monthly technical review meeting (MTRM), new technologies and crop varieties are discussed and agreed upon for adoption. These are then passed down to the smallholder farmers through the extension services agents. Below the ADPEX and the PMU are the extension services units whose main function is the dissemination of technical information to the peasant farmers participating in the programme. In theory, the extension unit's staff are the link between the project management and the farmers. These extension officers are expected to convey the needs of peasant farmers to the MTRM. But in practice, the extension staff often act independently of the MTRM thereby complicating the delivery system and alienating potential peasant farmers from the programme.

Ironically, peasant farmers themselves were not represented in those meetings despite the fact that it was their livelihood that was being discussed and decided upon. When this researcher asked the officer about the lack of involvement of the peasant farmers in these monthly meetings, the officer's response was that such peasants' participation was irrelevant, and that their participation might disrupt the decision making process. The manager was of the opinion that the project administrators know what is best for the farmers, and therefore, their participation in the decision making process could only slow down the execution of the projects in the manner envisioned by ADPEC. He then went on to summarize the position of the project management thus:

> The rural farmer is the target. How do we help them out of their situation? We do this by taking to them relevant research information. We found that the only way we can reach these people is through the extension service agents. As regards their participation in the policy decision process, I don't think this is necessary because they have very little to contribute. We are here to help them out of their backward attitudes to farming (Interview, 1992).

The prevailing attitude at the agency, like at RISONPALM, is that the agency field workers know what is best for the farmers. For instance, peasants' desire for new technology and new crop varieties for adoption on personal plots, where food crops are grown, is routinely ignored by extension workers. The sheer commitment to improving productivity has blinded the management staff from the crucial social networks of cooperation under which peasants' production takes place.

There is no denying the fact that the extension agents are crucial to effecting the input delivery system to the smallholding farmers, however, their awkward relationship to the peasants, whom they were employed to help, often gets in the way of the technical delivery system. In fact, the extension services division employs the majority of staff working on the project sites statewide. The documents made available to us showed a ratio of one extension agent to 1,200 farmers (RISADEP Brief, agency publication). According to the media support officer at the agency, the extension agent selects a total of 64-100 contact farmers with whom he works. The underlying principle here is that through these contact farmers, the extension agents will be able to spread the new technologies to the rest of the peasant farmers in the project area. The farmers are divided into groups, and each group selects a representative with whom the extension officer works directly. In the following paragraphs we will outline the ways the delivery system operates.

Extension Area

RISADEP has 10 extension areas, 29 farming blocks and 177 farming circles. Each farming block is under the supervision of an extension agent who in turn reports to a block supervisor. The extension agent works directly with the contact farmer also known as cell representative. The outcome of the Monthly Technical Review Meeting (MTRM) is passed down to smallholder farmers by the extension agent through the contact farmers whose farms the agent uses as demonstration laboratories during the Training and Visitation (T & V) sessions. The T & V sessions are held twice a month, and at these sessions the agents relay to the farmers, production recommendations and new technologies that were introduced by the MTRM. The media and information officer outlined the mechanisms for establishing the relevance of these technologies to the farmers' particular needs thus:

> The development of new crops and technologies are normally undertaken by the resource persons at their various institutions. We tried this research multi-locationally to see how adaptable to the farmers' environment. Once it is o.k, we tell the farmers to do this and that (sic.), because it is going to better their life..... To do this, we have an army of workers on the field, who work constantly with the farmers and train them to change their outlook. There are conflicts (as regards adoption) because these people are traditional, and it is the duty of

these extension workers to break through these attitudes. (Interview; 1991).

The field day is a special occasion separate from the usual training and visitation (T & V) sessions that the agents routinely organized. The T & V sessions are occasions to recruit new farmers into the programme using every means possible, ranging from intimidation to indoctrination. On the surface, peasant farmers are usually given the opportunity to ask extension supervisors about the new technologies, new crops varieties, and benefits accruing from joining the project. As we noticed, this information was withheld from farmers who did not show any clear intention of joining the project.

The project manager acknowledged that there were problems with the differential treatment of various categories of peasant farmers to which we drew his attention. He nevertheless denied the allegations that the agency kept records of farmers who have been labelled "difficult" and "obstinate" by the extension agents. But the officer latter admitted that the field day is an occasion for "indoctrination, and occasion to openly praise farmers who had joined the project's experiment". He added that "you need to convince him (peasant farmer) of the superiority of your technology since the average farmer is very rigid." (Interview; 1991).

We found out that those peasants the officer referred to as "difficult" and "obstinate" were farmers who have challenged claims of the extension workers with regards to new technology. Indeed, the majority of the peasant farmers we talked to were suspicious of these new technologies, because they were rarely allowed to be used on the plots that were designated for growing food crops. New technologies were often restricted to farms of rich and middle peasants who concentrated mainly on commercial crops for export. The reason behind this is that the only way the agency could recover the cost of developing these new technologies is through advancing them to peasants who have the ability to pay the agency back in cash. For instance, most of the lower stratum peasants in our sample were excluded from the new technology, and they were not usually allowed to test new crop seedlings on their private plots.

The Smallholder Oil Palm Estate at Elele

Elele is an Ikwerre peasant community in Rivers State some forty kilometres from Port Harcourt. It is the nearest village to the Igbo community and a few kilometres away from one of the nation's crude petroleum deposits. The majority of the peasants here also traced their ancestry to Igbo mainland. During the colonial times, Elele became a province under the Port Harcourt municipal administration. Like Ubima, Elele was captured and annexed by the secessionist Biafran army because of its rich soil, and its nearness to Obangi, the main crude petroleum refinery school. It also harbours a substantial amount of crude petroleum which was being exploited by Elf and Agip oil corporations. Like Ubima, this community of 14,500 people was destroyed and its inhabitants forced to flee the area until after the end of the war in January of 1970. Because of the war, agricultural production came to a standstill during 1967 to 1970. Thus the area also became one of the peasant communities that qualified for the state agricultural revitalization programme.

RISONPALM and the Elele Mini-Estates

The project was previously managed by the defunct Eastern Nigerian Marketing Board (ENMB). After the State was carved out from the former Eastern Region at the outset of the civil war, the administration of the state's oil palm estate was transferred to the newly formed Rivers State Development Corporation (RSDC). In 1974, the RSDC was dissolved and replaced by the Agricultural Marketing Corporation which managed the project until 1978 when it was taken over by RISONPALM as part of the World Bank integrated rural development programme. The company inherited 3,049 hectares of oil palm, mainly of the old varieties from the Eastern Nigeria Development Corporation (ENDC). The company acquired 6,000 hectares of peasant land of which 4,000 has been planted to date. The project comes under phase II of the World Bank's ADP assistance programme with additional funding coming from the European Investment Bank which has to date provided $11 million in new funding. Like the Nucleus Estate, the smallholder project is expected to cover an area of 10,000 hectares of fully planted oil palm, and was supposed to provide 44% of the projected total output of 47,250 metric tons of palm oil and 10,126 metric tons of kernels when the project reached maturity in 1990 (bank document No.1525-UNI, 1978: 23).

Under the administration of RISONPALM, a 20 metric ton fruit bunches per hour (20 tons ffb/hr) miller was purchased and installed at the main estate for the sole use of the smallholder farmers. The company also retained the smallholding system which it inherited from the Agricultural Production

82

Marketing Board on the insistence of the World Bank. But the company was much more interested in the development of the more commercially viable Nucleus Estate at Ubima, and as a result, development on the smallholder project did not get off the ground until the early eighties.

The acquisition of additional peasants' land meant that a significant number of the peasant population became landless, and were therefore forced to seek employment at the main estate. According to the project executors, land acquisition will be compensated for by increased income to peasant farmers. Besides, an estimated 3,500 rural employment was envisaged once the project reached maturity. The project manager stated that the company paid five naira per hectare of land acquired which was way below the market value of the land at the time. Since most of the women could not be registered as head of households, compensation on land previously farmed by them were paid to their husbands. This exclusion of women from land ownership has its roots in the traditional values of the community which was exploited by the project's management for two reasons. First, if women lose land to the project, they could turn to the estate for employment where they will most definitely receive wages lower than those of men. Secondly, registering women as heads of households would offend the traditional rulers (chiefly class) who are charged with defending village morality, and who are also the main supporters of the ADPs.

Unlike the Nucleus Estate at Ubima where smallholder farmers were given technical advice and farm inputs in exchange for management's advice and purchase of peasants' output, the Elele smallholder farmers were allowed to manage their own plots. However, they are also required to bring the fresh fruit bunches (ffb) to the main estate for milling. This allows RISONPALM to appropriate peasants' surplus produce without direct intervention at the level of production. The peasants reacted to this exploitative practice by switching their plots away from production of export crops to food production. This also allowed them to engage in part-time wage work at the main estate without jeopardizing the production of food crop.

The company was very disappointed by peasants' reaction to its forced collectivization agenda. According to the assistant general manager, the company plans to increase its funding to the smallholder farmers. This will come in the form of technical advice and improved crop seedlings which according to the manager, is one way of ensuring that the independent smallholder farmers produce commercial crops. The impression we got from talking to management staff was that it would like to run the Elele like a private enterprise as it did with the Ubima

Nucleus Estate. But peasants' resistance continues to delay this process of massive capitalization.

In the community as a whole, there is a sense of deep resentment towards the management staff. Peasant farmers complained that the extension agents treated them with little or no respect. The chief claimed that most of the amenities we saw in the community were secure through community efforts and without the financial support of the project administration. The sense of alienation within the community was expressed through several means including but not limited to destruction of the project's property, theft of company's fresh fruit bunches, trespassing, and frequent physical attacks on the staff of the project administration. In response to these peasants' protest, the company has increased security at the estate. Villagers are routinely refused access to the perimeters of the main estate. RISONPALM sought permission from the state government to raise its own security force to parade the perimeter of the estate but this was refused. It is not unusual to see groups of vigilante youths recruited by the company to harass and intimidate the villagers. Most of the youths, we were told, were recruited from the surrounding villages.

In a sense, the social structure at Elele is less rigid when compared to that of the Ubima village where the project administrators were able to buy off the chiefs in exchange for unlimited acquisition of peasants' land. Indeed, the traditional chief in Elele was equally as ferocious in his denunciation of the project administrators. Since the running of the smallholder project was taken over by RISADEP, it has re-adjusted its activities at Elele by encouraging independent peasant smallholder farmers to form their own cooperatives. RISADEP provided extension services advice to the farmers in addition to familiarizing them with new technologies and new crop varieties. It has also encouraged the peasants to sell their crops to independent millers without the repercussion of losing technical and other support from the agency. In addition to this, the agency has also encouraged the formation of a Women in Agriculture Programme which allows women to form their own cooperatives without having to seek permission from their husbands. The establishment of the Women in Agriculture Programme, as a component of the smallholder project, was in response to increased militancy on the part of peasant women, some of whom had refused to allow their plots to be taken over by RISONPALM.

The Better Life for Rural Women, a national women movement, has also succeeded in re-focusing the agency strategy to include mobilizing women for national development through increased literary education for peasant women participating in the programme. The women's movement has also begun to challenge the long standing tradition of assigning subordinate roles to women, by organizing weekend schools for women where they receive training in all sorts of arts ranging from crafts, numeracy education, small business education and domiciliary nursing training.

The Women in Agriculture Programme and The Better Life for Rural Women Movement have heightened the tension between the elders and young women in the village. This tension has led to the formation of an informal alliance between women and young men in an effort to fight the oligarchy of older men. But they have also extended their efforts towards fighting the encroaching tendencies of international finance institutions. The newly found independence of peasant women is clearly a challenge to the project administrators and village elders alike. With the exception of market women, who are traditionally independent of their husbands, the majority of women in our sample clearly agreed that the current direction and the definition of the project goals should be re-examined. But the project management continues to capitalize on the different levels of conflicts at the two project villages for its own purpose. In the next chapter we turn our attention and analysis to our control village, Aluu.

6 The Village of Aluu: The Control Village

Location and Characteristics

Aluu village is about 25 kilometres from Port Harcourt and is one of the oldest peasant communities in Ikwerre. This community of about 6,000 people has not lost any of the communal land to the projects, as have the two project villages of Ubima and Elele. The only sign of modernity is the federal University of Port Harcourt, located in the village and which has contributed very little to improving living conditions in the area. A proposal to set up an alternative energy research programme that would involve the community here was killed by administrators who could not see the essence of ivory tower professors interacting with peasant farmers.

The name Aluu means "to fight", a reflection of the warlike attitude of the community. There are ten villages in the community; Omuchuolu, Omuoda, Mbando, Omuike, Omuoko, Omuahunwo, Omuhuechi, Omuokiri and Omuigwe. We randomly selected three households from each of the ten villages for this study. The main occupation of this community is subsistence farming. A few of the peasant farmers are engaged in commercial farming in such crops as oil palm, raffia palm, and root crops which are the major sources of cash.

Economic Activities

At the end of the planting season, some members of the community engage in hunting and petty commerce to supplement family income while waiting for their crops to be ready for harvesting. While men engage in hunting and other odd jobs during the end of the planting season, women continue to farm on family plots to grow food to support the entire family. Land allocation for this type of activity is

86

less rigid than commercial farming since any member of the clan, irrespective of gender, could clear a portion of the common land that has being lying fallow for a period of time. There is no private ownership of land. Land allocated to each family unit could not be sold, exchanged or put forward as collateral.

At the main village market, women set up sheds to sell surplus food they produce, and also sell game that is brought home by their menfolk. The village market is not only the place where the exchange of commodities takes place, it is also the arena where social interaction and networking among women are effected. The central nexus of women's social interaction is the Sunday market which is held every other week. At the Sunday market important social relations are carried out. The market also provides the occasion for women from all the ten villages to meet and organize village activities ranging from marriage brokerage, naming ceremony, and reflection on matters affecting them both at the village and the clan's levels. One village elder told me that if you want to hear about village matters, the Sunday market is the right place to go because it is there where gossiping takes place. Because women are by tradition excluded from the village assembly, the market has become the most important avenue for women to organize and exercise their political power.

Unlike Ubima and Elele, production for exchange is not as widespread in Aluu but increasingly becoming so. The commodification of social relations and the moneterization of the subsistent peasant economy are on a relatively small scale compared with those at project villages of Elele and Ubima. At village markets in Ubima and Elele, new trading elites have sprung up since the arrival of the projects. They dominate and control exchange relations between peasant producers and the commodity buyers. Exchange relations at Ubima and Elele are transacted entirely through the medium of money, whereas at Aluu, villagers still bring their goods to the market either to sell or exchange for other goods of comparable value. In short, there is a partial commodification at Aluu compared to the total commodification that has taken place at Ubima and Elele.

In Aluu, most farming activities are still carried out on the family plots, which in most cases, is less than half of a hectare. A household's annual income is around 2,100 naira. Peasant farmers still rely entirely on their family labour working under the most appalling conditions. For example the majority of peasants here still rely on the traditional hoe and cutlass. Rarely did this researcher run into farmers who were using modern equipment comparable to those at the project villages. Most of the peasant farmers in our sample still rely on the knowledge of the elders for deciding upon the planting time. Some rich farmers hire labour to work on their farms all year round. Most of the labourers we interviewed came from upland Igboland or from other nearby villages where land alienation has been going on as a result of land seizure by both multinational corporations and ADPs' administrators.

Gerontocracy and the System of Distribution

Like most peasant communities in south eastern Nigeria, Aluu village is highly patriarchal with political authority monopolized by male members of the clan. The seeming resistance of this traditional community to change may be explained by the rigidity of its social structure. At the top of the social hierarchy are older members of the clan who made up what is known as the council of elders.

The council of elders is made up of titled and untitled chiefs, and older male members who have earned membership into the council because of their age. Titled chiefs are chiefs who are descendants of clan chiefs and they have acquired the titles as a result of the death of their fathers who previously held the positions of traditional chiefs. On the other hand, there are other titled chiefs who have distinguished themselves in selfless service to the clan or those members who have migrated to the urban centres, and who have achieved wealth through trading. Some of these buy their titles in order to boost their social standing in the community. Some members of this class were simply awarded the chieftaincy for their outstanding achievement outside of the traditional hierarchy.

In terms of the overall social relations within the clan, the council of elders generally oversees its moral code and rules of genealogy, especially with regards to marriage and clan members' sexual practices. They also monopolize such things as the knowledge of the planting seasons including certain days of the year that are prohibited from planting. The Aluu village tradition also encourages communal sharing. For example, peasant's household produce is divided into two parts. The first part consists of those items that are designated for the immediate reproduction of the household.

The second part is the surplus which is normally made available to the community common fund. From this fund, older members of the clan, who can no longer support themselves or without relatives to lean on, are usually taken care off. The rules of reciprocation guiding this surplus fund are strictly guarded and enforced by the council of elders. In most cases, younger members of the clan, with very little family responsibility, contribute more to this fund than any other members of the clan. In general, male members can marry as many wives as they are able to support. Rich peasants, in particular, indulge in polygamy as a means of expanding the labour supply on their farms. Many Aluu women also engage in polyandrous relationships, especially first daughters of chiefs, who by tradition cannot be bethroned outside of the clan. In most cases, polyandrous practices are simply the result of high bride price. We shall discuss this more fully in the proceeding chapter.

The Survey

Like the two project villages, 30 peasant's households were surveyed. Each household head, and additional adult members of the household were interviewed. The typical division of labour within the household is one in which the male adults farm family plots which are usually a few kilometers from the centre of the compound. Farming practices are still traditional. The dominant farming equipments are the cutlasses and hoes. Unlike the two project villages, modern equipments and application of fertilizers are still very rarely in use. In the majority of the cases in our sample, bush fallow system is the preferred form of farming. Usually, a particular crop is planted for one or two seasons, then the family moves to another portion of the plot leaving the land fallow for several planting seasons before finally returning to it. This practice does not allow for effective and economic planting of the land.

Similarly, because very few fertilizers are used by the farmers, the top soil often deteriorates so rapidly to the extent that after a few years of tenancy, the plots are abandoned altogether. The main cash crops in Aluu are oil palm, raffia palm and palm kernel. Normally, some of these crops take, on the average between 5-10 years to grow (from planting to harvesting), depending on the crop variety. As a result, many adult members in Aluu village often engage in indolent practices while waiting for the crops to be ready for harvest. In the course of this research, we came across many able bodied young men who spent their time either playing or simply getting drunk on the native liquor - *Tombo*. In fact, the level of alcoholism is far greater in this control village than in the two other project villages.

In almost all the households in our sample, there were usually two to four elderly members of the family who had come to live with their sons or daughters for security purposes. These were either the parents of the wife, or elder sisters of the husband who had returned to the village because of the loss of their husbands. In Igbo tradition, as we shall examine in detail in chapter six, women who married

89

under the small dowry marriage arrangement were bound, by tradition, to return to their father's compound once their husbands passed away. Having two generations living under the same roof as we encountered in Aluu is a very serious economic burden. This may explain the low standard of living and income compared to the two project villages. In all, able bodied men who can work are bound by tradition to support the older generation. In our Aluu sample, older adult members represent nearly 20-30 percent of the household, whereas in Ubima and Elele, the figure is under 15 percent. This may be due in part to the fact that the older generation, particularly women who lost their husbands, could easily get jobs in the main estate at the project villages, or join one of the cooperatives established by the project's administrators.

Women and Farming

From the analysis of our household sample for Aluu village, it became clear that women are the backbone of the rural economy, providing the necessary subsistence for the entire family. While land for commercial farming is usually a long distance away from the centre of the compound, land for food crops is usually available in the vicinity of the village. The restriction on common land, when it comes to growing food, is not as strict as the case for cash crop. Most adult women in the household and their grown up daughters, usually keep small plots scattered over the surroundings of the village. In so far as no one is currently planting any food crops in adjoining land, the women are free to convert such plots for their temporary use. These women grow basic food staples like cassava, millet, yam, plantain and cocoyam. The women also are responsible for processing the cassava into gari which is the most commonly consumed item in the village.

The process of refining cassava could be very laborious, requiring patience and skills which only women dominate. Generally, on each family plot, each peasant household produces food in excess of their needs. The reason for this is to enable them to acquire money to buy other food items such as fish and other sea food items which are produced by the riverine peasant farmers. It is not unusual to have the eldest female members of the household raising poultry in the backyards. Markets are held twice a week. The mid-week market is generally held on Wednesday during which women bring their yams, plantains and assorted vegetables to sell for cash to civil servants and staff of the University of Port Harcourt, which is just a few metres away from the village.

The Sunday village is much more elaborate than the mid-week market.

90

This is held in the Choba market place, an area specifically designated by village elders for that purpose. Women bring their processed cassava (gari) to exchange for cash or barter for fish, while men sell locally brewed liquor to Ijaw traders. In our sample, women generally bring home more than three quarters of the household income, and this comes mainly from the sales of processed cassava. Older women, especially those who can still work, set up stores in the centre of the village selling wares such as cigarettes, home brewed liquor and imported goods that found their way into the community through younger men who travelled to the city centre. At least 75 percent of women in our Aluu sample said they routinely engaged in one form of trading to complement their family income. Many of the women also spent more time attending to family matters than most women in the project village. Those engaged in multiple cohabitations spent different days of the week with concubines in adjoining villages. This form of polyandry relationships, even though not officially sanctioned at the clan level, is still widespread in Aluu.

Esusu and Collective Work

One important characteristics of the Aluu village is the enduring tradition of the village communal life which has almost disappeared in the project villages. Women meet once every month in the house of a member. At these meetings, food and drinks are provided by the person in whose house the meeting is being held. At the end of the meeting, each member contributes money to the common fund. This fund generally goes to the member in whose house the meeting was held. In most cases, such money is used by the member either to set herself up in small business, or pay off debts incurred due to the loss of a father or mother. The meeting then moves to the house of the next member who is also entitled to the contributions the next time round. This practice of communal lending is based partly on trust, and the rate of default, this researcher was told, is very minimal. In case of death of a member, the debt is often taken over by the oldest daughter of the deceased, or in the absence of such a sibling, the members of the Esusu bear the loss. The Esusu is symbolic in the sense that it serves as a form of mechanical solidarity among members of the clan, most especially the female members, much in the same way as collective work spirit among male members.

While the women engage themselves in the practice of Esusu, men also carry out similar social relations. In Aluu tradition, the older boy of the household must leave the family hut once he reaches puberty and is eligible to take a wife.

Generally, the clan head assigns a plot for the new eligible bachelor. Since he belongs to an age-grade, the burden of building a new hut falls on the shoulders of the members of the age grade. Collective work like this, tends to create the basis for village solidarity. The collective work spirit is often extended to communal farming, and are often exploited by older members of the clan who control the rule of bethronement.

The absence of a regular work routine may account for the persistence of this age old practice among the Aluu villagers. In Ubima and Elele, job openings in the plantations and the cooperative farms, have made it impossible for the system of collective work to endure as we shall discuss fully in the following chapter. The state government's desire to extend the rural integrated programme state wide may also be the surest way of combatting the sort of indolence that this researcher ran into in this peasant village. Surely, the introduction of a new division of labour, which the ADPs would obviously bring about, may go a long way to reduce the burden of work on women.

The persistence of old habits, even though Aluu village is already integrated into the modern economy, still remains to be explained. The impression this researcher got was that the fact that the villagers could easily reproduce themselves even on the simple labour of their womenfolk may explain the resistance to, and hostility to change. While the farmers here agreed that they would like to enjoy the benefits of improved seedlings, extension advice and modern farm inputs, yet they were very suspicious of the developer's intent.

In the sample, resistance to the ADPs is often stronger among older men who perhaps see a serious threat to their traditional authority. Those women who opposed the ADPs did so for fear that they would lose whatever skills they presently possess, most especially, in the area of cassava processing. The dominant economic role of women within Aluu society is their strongest asset. But despite such dominance, Aluu women continue to experience a subordinate role within the households and in the clan in general.

Crude Petroleum and Environmental Pollution in the Project Area

One of the most disturbing patterns in the project area is environmental pollution. As mentioned earlier, southeast Nigeria is the centre of crude petroleum exploration. For years, the ecology and environment in this area have been subject to degradation by the activities of crude oil multinational corporations without any state intervention. As we also alluded earlier on, the sudden found wealth in crude petroleum led the Nigerian state to focus its development policies on the urban sector of the economy while paying very little attention to environmental destruction that crude petroleum exploration naturally embodies. The crude petroleum based industrialization based strategy of the Nigerian state also meant a close cooperation between foreign oil multinationals and regulatory agencies of the Nigerian state. However, because of its subordinate position vis a vis the oil multinationals, the Nigerian state could not enforce safety standards that would protect both the environment and people living in the oil producing areas. The result of this was a massive destruction of peasants' farmlands, and extensive pollution of fishing ponds that peasant farmers rely upon for their livelihood especially around the riverine areas. This pollution comes directly from frequent crude spillages and oil blowouts (Badru, 1985).

For example on January 17th, 1980, the Nigerian oil industry experienced its worst disaster when Texaco's Funiwa 5 oil well blew out, setting 321 peasant villages ablaze. The blowout lasted for thirteen days before Texaco finally got its emergency response force from the United States to put the blaze under control. The damage to peasants' lives and property was extensive. It was reported that 230,000 barrels of crude was spilled during the thirteen days blowout polluting 1,200 square miles of coastline, mangrove swamps, rivers and creeks. In the five villages most affected by the blowout - Koluama I, Koluama II, Fishtown, Sagana and Otuofor - 180 deaths were recorded, 3,000 farmers were treated with oil related ailments while nearly a quarter of a million villagers were displaced (see Hutchful, 1985:9-56).

Despite the seriousness of the accident, especially the permanent loss of livelihood to several villagers in the area where the blowout occurred, the Nigerian government refused to put pressure on Texaco to give adequate compensation to villagers in the affected area. To date, there is no concrete evidence to suggest that Texaco and Shell, for that matter, have improved their safety standards in the light of the Texaco's Funiwa 5 blowout. In fact, over the past ten years, Shell has recorded numerous oil spills that one could barely keep record of as I will elaborate below. However, the insensitivity demonstrated towards these peasants' communities by state bureaucrats clearly shows the contradictions of dependent development.

It is this sort of frequent oil related accident, continuous gas flaring, pond pollution, and other ecological disasters in the area that of recent fuelled community based agitations towards crude oil multinationals. But the Nigerian state's response to the continuing destruction of the environment in the oil producing communities was to tighten its control and surveillance of local opposition leaders, resulting in gross abuse and violation of basic rights.

In Ogoniland for example, oil exploration has led to a total collapse of this community. Ogoniland is one of the many communities in southeast Nigeria where oil drilling started some 35 years ago by Shell - the Dutch crude petroleum conglomerate. The two main oil multinationals in the area are Shell and Texaco, and both of them have very poor safety records (Badru, 1984). In fact, the first refinery was established at Eleme, the heartland of the Ogoni people. For 35 years, Shell and other small oil companies, have lifted crude petroleum from Ogoniland to the tune of $30 billion dollars. Currently, Shell makes an annual profit of $170 million from its operation in this community alone. A small community of only 400 square miles, comprising of 321 peasant villages with a total population of 250,000 peasant farmers, Oginoland is home to 96 oil wells and five big pumping stations (cf. New York Times, February 13, 1996).

Today, Shell pumps 900,000 barrels of crude petroleum from this area out of which it pockets 257, 000 barrels, nearly a third, before delivering the rest to the rentier Nigerian state. Despite its oil riches, Ogoniland is the most backward area in Nigeria, and the most ecologically polluted of all the oil producing communities. Since oil exploration began in the area in the early sixties, local fish farming has been totally destroyed while constant crude oil spills have turned the land virtually barren. In addition, ceaseless gas flaring has also made, and continues to make, life unbearable especially for farmers whose villages are located next to the flaring stations. Reports of birth deformities, complications during childbirth, and abnormally high miscarriage rates reported amongst women of childbearing age, are but a few serious medical calamities that have befallen this community since Shell started its operation here. During one of my visits to the oil producing areas in the early eighties, it was not uncommon to see villagers drawing drinking water from polluted ponds (Badru, 1984). Efforts to get Shell to provide portable water to villagers in the area was frustrated by Shell officials who did not see such provision as part of their concerns.

Between 1976 and 1980, there have been 784 reported incidents of crude oil spills involving 1,336,875 barrels of crude oil. Despite the frequency of these accidents, Shell showed very little concern at the ecological impact of the oil spills on the community. Indeed, Shell was on record as saying that it was not its responsibility to show concerns for the environment (New York Times, February 13, 1996). It has also been reported that Shell pays very little attention to safety standards, especially in the developing countries where it has its operations compared to similar operations in Europe and North America. It was this sort of destruction and the intransigence on the part of Shell plus Shell's official refusal to listen to complaints from villagers that led to the recent political and social turmoils that finally resulted in the execution of several environmentalists in the era.

There is a clear relationship between the World Bank funded ADPs in the area and crude oil exploration. The ability of the Nigerian state to get loans from both the World Bank, and IMF, is simply based on the continuing exploitation and sales of crude. In other words, the credit worthiness of the Nigerian state is based on continuous oil exploitation without which loans for agricultural development would not have been made available. There is a certain irony in all of this because some of the rural development projects in the area have to cope with ecological destruction of peasants' crops due to ceaseless gas flaring. In the end what the World Bank tries to build, the oil corporations destroy.

In the following chapter, I will discuss the result of our findings. The two project villages of Ubima and Elele are discussed first, and then we compare the two project villages to the control village of Aluu. Perhaps I should state once again, that the three villages were part of the same municipality before the civil war. Pre-project income and conditions were fairly similar. Terrains and climatic conditions are also similar, and whatever variations that may exist, geologically speaking, are so inconsequential that they can hardly influence or account for the differences discovered in this survey.

7 Discussion of Findings

The three villages surveyed for this book provided us with some interesting insights into the impact of the agricultural modernization programme on the social structure of these peasants' communities. In this section we discuss and compare the data we collected in the three villages. The village of Aluu is where our control sample was drawn from, and it was chosen because none of the Agricultural Development Projects (ADP) have yet been implemented in the area. Aluu also presents us with a good choice, because it is a village that combines a lot of the characteristics of our experimental villages - Ubima and Elele. The Aluu village is also believed to be the centre of Ikwere culture where traditional Igbo attitudes are very much in abundance. The choice of Aluu was also determined by the familiarity of this researcher with the area. As a result of this familiarity, the villagers were much more comfortable with our interviews and our presence in the village did not cause panic to villagers who were traditionally suspicious of government officials.

Economic Impact of the ADPs

The impact on the villages over a ten year period will be discussed under three broad headings. These are: economic impact, sociological impact and changes in social relations as they relate to the process of class formation. Traditionally, evaluation of the bank's projects are usually restricted to their economic impact, but it is the belief of this author that such economistic analysis often ignores fundamental changes in social relations that could not be washed under mathematical figures. Contrary to this practice, the discussion of the findings will focus under two areas namely, the economic and the sociological analyses.

Economic Prosperity: Change or "Tradition"?

From the analysis of the data collected in the three villages, there is a convincing evidence that the ADPs have made, and continue to make tremendous social and economic impact on the communities where the projects are located. Whether these changes are positive or negative is a matter of which approach one takes. In particular, the understanding of the overall changes in the social structure that the projects have facilitated will provide us with a clear understanding of the contradictory effects of externally influenced social change. The overall emphasis of our analysis will be on social transformation at the clan level. In this regard, the effects of the projects can be seen most poignantly in the traditional institutions of these peasant villages, most of which are now giving way to forces of change, while at the same time retaining their own peculiar dynamics.

Ubima

The indicators used in measuring these changes include among others, household income, infant mortality, life expectancy, access to portable water, health provision, access to motorable roads, and birth control practices. Overall, in the three villages surveyed, our data clearly showed that Ubima, where the Nucleus Estate is located, has been transformed most compared to the other villages. On the average, a typical peasant's household annual income calculated from income received from sales of farm produce, and those earned as wage labourer at the main estate, is far higher than those of the peasant farmers in the villages of Elele and Aluu. The average household income in the peasant village of Ubima, for example, is 3,400 naira annually which is higher than those at Elele and Aluu village.

Existing government household income survey shows a pre-project average income for the three villages of between 600 and 1,600 naira most of which is accrued from subsidence farming (bank document No. 1525-UNI, 1978: 25). Similarly, infant mortality rate is lower in Ubima in comparison to the other villages. In Elele and Aluu, average income is 3,150 and 2,100 naira respectively. In the project area infant mortality is around 10 deaths in 1,000 births whereas in the non project village of Allu, it is around 15 which is equal to the national average in 1989 (World Bank, 1991:256). Average life expectancy at Ubima is around 68 years, whereas at Elele, the second project village, average life

97

expectancy is slightly above 56 years. In Aluu, the infant mortality rate is still higher than those for Ubima and Elele, and average life expectancy here is less than 50 years (RISADEP data, 1992).

The difference in both infant mortality rate and the life expectancy is explained by increasing access to improved medical facilities by villagers at the project village, especially the Nucleus Estate. Access to medical care is also being facilitated because of improved road networks, the availability of regular health information pamphlets provided by the extension workers, and visitation by the state's domiciliary nurses. In most of the 30 households surveyed, at Ubima there is either a pipe bore water device or mono-pumps located in the centre of the clan. This access to portable water may also account for the differences in life expectancy, and the differential in infant mortality rate reported above. There is also an increased awareness among villagers at Nucleus Estate in Ubima about general cleanliness, and about the importance of reporting an outbreak of any communicable diseases to the nearby clinics. This awareness is reflected in the number of reported visits to the main medical centre which is greater than the number of visits made by villagers in our control village. Indeed, such visits by villagers in our control sample were often hampered by poor road facilities and the lower level of health care awareness.

Finally, reproductive awareness and family planning are also much more widespread, and increasingly becoming part of the village life at Elele and Ubima. In contrast, in the village of Aluu such practices as family planning and safe sex are still discountenanced by village elders. Discussion about reproductive sexuality is still guided by age old tradition and taboos. In the control village of Aluu, reproductive rights are still determined by the older male members of the community while women's main role continued to be associated with reproducing the clan. In fact, women in the control village have very little control over the procreative process, and the percentage of women of child bearing age, as a percentage of all women, is higher than those in the project villages. Nationally, the percentage of women of childbearing age as a percentage of all women in 1989 was 43 (World Bank; ibid). When this survey was done, the percentage of women of married age as percentage of total women in the project areas has fallen dramatically to 35 percent, while it still remains as high as 45 percent in the control village. The reason behind this, as will be pointed out later in this chapter, is that more and more younger women are getting gainful employment at the Nucleus Estate while deferring marriage until later years.

In Ubima, traditional taboos about procreative sexuality are being challenged by the extension workers as well as radical activists of the grassroots women organization called Better Life for Rural Women (BLRW), whose offices provide counselling for peasant women about reproductive rights and available family planning options. The BLRW is a national organization of women focusing on poverty among rural women in addition to improving their literacy level. This organization has contributed more to raising women's awareness than the project itself. However, the local women activists have used the infrastructure created by the project to achieve their goals.

Elele

At Elele, average household income at the time of this survey was 3,150 naira, not too far behind those at the Ubima Nucleus Estate. The pre-project average income in Elele, like in Ubima, was around 600 naira. The income of most households comes from sales of commercial crops grown on family plots and from income derived from regular and seasonal employment from RISONPALM plantation. The majority of the wage earners within a typical household are women who lost their farms to the project administration. Indeed, 65 percent of all agricultural workers in the project area are women. These women also supplement household income from trading which is organized around the buying and selling of surplus food crops produced by upper and middle peasant families. The data collected also showed that women, and young men between the ages of 15-30, constituting 45 percent of all peasant households, also bring home nearly 85 percent of household income.

In the two project villages of Elele and Ubima, the number of children of age range 8-12 years taking part in family production or actively engaged in full time paid employment is significantly smaller than that of Aluu where young children still play a vital role in family reproduction. This is due partly to the expansion of community schools in the project villages. Many children spent most of their time at the community schools as opposed to spending time as farm hands on their family plots. Cooperatives farms, in the project villages, discourage the use of child labour, however several under age children still work on family plots during out of school hours. Usually family plots still remain the units for household reproduction employing mainly child and female labour especially younger females not considered ready for marriage.

Older members of the households are supported from family income earned by women and young men. At our control village, most older men of age

99

70-85 years continue to maintain their own plots which they farm regularly for subsistence. At Ubima and Elele, the opportunity for paid employment at the project sites allows for younger members of the family to earn wages sufficient to support older members of the family. Indeed, moderate access to farm equipments, fertilizers and new varieties of crop seedlings allowed peasant farmers at Elele and Ubima to spend less time on family plots. Upper and middle peasantry increasingly spend their newly found leisure time in making handicrafts, and attending communal meetings which are held every week.

The Impact of Structural Adjustment Programme (SAP)

The introduction of structural adjustment programme (SAP) officially in the mid-eighties has almost wiped out the economic benefits brought to the project's communities by the ADPs. In late 1986, the military government of General Ibrahim Babangida announced a series of policy guidelines which were designed to re-adjust the national economy. But these polices were exact replicas of those prescribed by the World Bank and the International Monetary Fund under the structural adjustment programme designed to revive the faltering economy.

The structural adjustment programme (SAP) contains nine fiscal guidelines or what the bank official's chose to dub as "conditionalities". The idea is that once these guidelines are followed, member states adopting the programme will automatically qualify for new line of credit from the IMF to re-adjust their economies. These infamous "conditionalities" can be summarized briefly as follows:

1. devaluation of the national currency and the abolition of foreign exchange control.

2. fiscal anti-inflationary policies that call for removal of subsidies on essential items including petroleum.

3. reduction of state spending on social services such as health and education.

4. trade liberalization; maintaining open door to investment and importation of foreign goods.

100

5. privatization of public enterprises (parastatals) and sale of government shares in private companies.

6. open door policy for multinational corporations including free repatriation of accumulated profits.

7. monetary anti-inflationary polices, including but not limited to control of bank lending and higher interest rates.

8. control and reduction of wages paid to labour.

9. anti-inflationary dismantling of price control and minimum wages.

In short, these policy recommendations by the IMF, and evidently supported by the World Bank, continue to generate disastrous consequences for the economy. The underlying assumption of the bank's adjustment policy is that by implementing its key fiscal policies, it will automatically correct the imbalance within the economy while at the same time boosting peasant productivity, and re-arranging the sectoral balance between the urban and rural sectors in favour of the latter. The devaluation of the national currency, the argument goes, will generate export capacity, improve optimal use of resources, and more importantly, increasing the amount of income paid to peasant farmers which historically had been pegged down by government bureaucrats. This adjustment reasoning will hold water only if the national economy itself reflects internal coherence between different sectors, and without external connection to foreign markets that are constantly manipulated by multinational corporations.

Indeed, several scholars have shown that where these policies have been executed in the Third World, the opposite effects have been achieved. Instead of improving the condition of the national economy, structural adjustment policies of the bank have sunk several Third World nations deeper into crisis and, into national catastrophes that often undermined the stability of the state (Hutchful, 1989). It has also been shown that these polices have complicated the efforts towards sustained development in the developing countries of the south in addition to actually blocking the prospect of internally generated development dynamics (Onimade, 1988; Hutchful, 1990). Since my concern here is to show how these policies have impacted on rural communities in the project area, I shall

101

restrict my discussion of SAP to the economic impact of currency devaluation and its impact on peasants' productivity, and on peasants' household incomes which have dramatically declined since the implementation of the programme.

The impact of SAP is most dramatic in connection with the exchange rate of the national currency, the naira. In the seventies, when the first set of ADPs were adopted by the Rivers State government, the Nigerian national currency was exchanging at almost one naira to one U.S. dollar, and three naira to one British pound sterling. At the time, inputs such as fertilizers, trucks and herbicides were moderately priced and accessible to most categories of peasant farmers. At the time this field work was undertaken in 1991, the naira was exchanging at the rate of 10 to one U.S. dollar, and 25 naira to one British pound sterling.

Since the conclusion of this study, the Nigerian currency has fallen sharply, and currently the official exchange rate is 20 naira to one U.S. dollar (UBA, Economic Monthly Business and Economic Digest, Lagos, Vol. 15 (3), 1992:1). Ever since, the currency has steadily depreciated to the amazement of government officials who originally praised the implementation of the adjustment programme. Today the naira is currently exchanging at the rate of 84 naira to one U.S. dollar. Prices of basic consumer commodities have in most cases risen more than 100 percent, while wages remain at the pre-SAP levels. The average wage remains at less than 15,000 naira (U.S. $125) for middle class income earners, while the inflation rate has quadrupled in the past five years.

In the project area, weighted household income is ten times less than the pre-project era. The following table shows the escalating cost of living since the introduction of the structural adjustment programme (SAP). The figures focused on major cities where escalating prices continue to put pressure on government services and quality of life. In many cities some major food items have become so scarce that the government has resorted to rationing. Long lines of workers in major cities were in evidence while we were collecting data for this book. Except for the military officers who received a monthly allocation of essential food items, workers in urban cities have to do without basic food essential for their diets.

In the rural areas, conditions were even worst as prices escalated beyond the reach of the average farmers whose post-project purchasing power has been tremendously reduced by triple digit inflation. Urban workers with roots in the rural enclaves, routinely return to relatives to supplement their incomes, thereby putting additional pressure on the village's meagre resources. Most villagers interviewed generally complained about the harsh and inhuman conditions created by the government's adoption of the adjustment programme.

Table 7.1: Combined Urban and Rural State Consumer Price Index (Base Period: September 1985 = 100)

State	Dec.1989 Food	Dec.1989 All Items	Nov.1990 Food	Nov.1990 All Items	Dec.1990 Food	Dec.1990 All Items
Akwa	333.3	286.5	333.7	294.3	338.0	297.7
Anambra	307.4	287.2	307.5	307.4	311.6	310.4
Bauchi	295.9	286.1	280.8	282.8	279.5	283.4
Bendel	354.3	309.6	348.4	321.8	351.5	326.8
Benue	398.2	354.7	417.3	383.5	331.4	323.1
Borno	248.2	250.1	299.0	297.2	301.5	299.3
Cross R.	298.2	278.7	267.7	270.0	276.8	273.2
Gongola	284.7	267.3	331.7	305.5	338.7	309.0
Imo	441.6	366.8	323.4	297.0	342.4	310.9
Kaduna	264.6	244.2	306.2	274.7	297.9	274.0
Katsina	248.3	269.2	282.0	276.1	275.2	273.0
Kano	204.8	211.3	239.8	237.9	234.6	236.0
Kwara	426.1	376.8	361.7	329.8	375.0	342.2
Lagos	294.2	288.9	297.1	308.2	306.2	318.7
Niger	249.9	252.6	250.5	259.2	244.4	257.7
Ogun	353.3	318.6	323.2	295.3	321.6	296.0
Ondo	337.9	296.6	351.3	312.2	361.3	320.5
Oyo	299.1	292.0	307.2	309.3	298.7	305.9
Plateua	241.3	245.1	250.6	252.3	271.4	267.5
Rivers	330.8	304.3	368.9	357.7	399.7	379.5
Sokoto	244.9	242.5	256.3	245.1	279.7	264.1

Source: Reproduced from the United Bank for Africa's Monthly Business and Economic Digest, Vol.14, No.3, March 1991, p.8.

The impact of the project on peasant's income as we discussed above, despite the rising cost of living and the inflationary effect is appreciable compared to the non-project communities in the area. However, the implementation of the adjustment programme has almost wiped out the gains of the projects. For instance, basic food items in both rural and urban centres have quadrupled in price since the implementation of the SAP under the most repressive regime of General

Ibrahim Babangida. Urban dwellers, especially those living on fixed incomes and without alternative sources of income like trading and petty-contracting have suffered most under the structural adjustment programme. In addition to this, SAP has also brought unusual burden on the operations of government. For example, most government ministries are routinely deserted as hungry employees abandon their jobs to engage in petty trading in the informal sector of the economy.

While the economic impact of the ADPs showed significant disparities between project and non-project villages, the programme has its most profound and devastating sociological effects on the social structure of these communities. In fact, some of the effects of the projects on the villages selected for this study were not actually intended as we shall see later in this section. One significant element of all of these is that some of the changes brought about by the projects posed serious challenge to both the project administrators and community leaders whose authority is increasingly being challenged.

Changes in Social Relations

While the findings above with regards to the economic impact of the projects did not come as a surprise, the tremendous impact on social relations and social institutions represented the most significant findings of this research. In the course of this fieldwork, attention was paid to three aspects of village life which we believed would provide us with the information as to what extent the projects have intruded on the village community. The institutions selected for discussion here are; clan authority structure, the marriage system and the institution of collective (communal) work. All three are important African institutions which have remained almost intact in spite of more than a century of colonial contact. In addition to this, this concluding section will look at the class differentiation that the project had promoted in the two communities.

Sociological Impact of the ADPs

I. Clan Authority Pattern

In "Modernization: Protest and Change", Eisenstadt argues that the undemocratic traditional authority, and political structures which characterize most non-industrial societies are major impediments to political and economic modernization (Eisenstadt, 1966). The dominance of gerontocratic authority, Eisenstadt argues, prevents the emergence of enterprising spirit and innovative minds. In pre-industrial societies, these qualities of free enterprise and innovative approach to the environment are most likely to be repressed by age old tradition, and adherence to taboos that continues to determine the clan's worldview. In order to overcome the condition of backwardness, Eisenstadt argues, the autocratic authority of the old society must be challenged by a social group whose vision is progressive and democratic.

In the three villages selected for this study, we found a direct relationship between the modernization of peasant agriculture and a growing threat to traditional authority patterns. In a typical Igbo social structure, the clan authority is constituted in the hands of the clan chief who is surrounded by the council of elders. The clan chief and the elders sanctioned what are morally acceptable, while political power is exercised through an elaborate system of gerontocratic rule. Under this system, the chief appoints the council of elders, comprising mainly oldest members of the clan, most of whom are male members of the household. At the bottom is the council of women, also made up of predominantly older women, and who by tradition do not take part in the decision making system. The council of women only acts as an advisory body to the clan chief. The chief's authority is given legitimacy by the members of the council of elders, and such authority is enforced by the "age grade system" of young able bodied men (18-35 years) who acted as the clan law enforcing body. The council of elders decides upon such things as the setting of bride price for eligible young women, and the setting of dates for communal ritual practices. The council also decides on the first day of the planting season, village ceremonies, work routine, settles disputes amongst clan folks, and the timing of intra-tribal wars.

Since the projects started, this study found that the clan chiefs and the council of elders have been losing their authority to the project administrators. In fact, the extension service officers now decide when the planting season begins. These agents of change, as they are popularly referred to in the project's office, are responsible for enforcing strict work ethics particularly among those peasants participating in the project. For example, the traditional practice of setting certain days of the planting season for ancestral worship has almost been abolished in Ubima and Elele. Whereas in the control village of Aluu, this traditional practice is still in force. Similarly, the practice of abandoning land for several years for ritual purposes or for fear of offending the ancestors is no longer allowed in the project villages. Indeed, such lands are usually taken over by extension workers who then use them as demonstration farms.

The chief's authority in Ubima and Elele is increasingly confined to areas which do not infringe upon the efficient performance of work by the villagers. In the project villages, there were reports of hostilities between the council of elders and the extension workers mainly because of the refusal of the extension workers to recognize the authority of the elders, which in Igbo tradition is an abomination. In many of these cases, the extension workers routinely win the battles against the elders, and many young men in the village increasingly seek planting advice from the younger extension officers. The result of this was the loss of traditional authority by the clan chief and the members of the council of elders. This loss of authority by the council of elders, the oldest village institution, is a clear indication of the triumph of the modernization efforts of the project.

The fear expressed most by villagers we interviewed in Aluu, our control village, is the fear of loss of tradition; a tradition that often alienates young men and women from their society. But what the elders are most afraid of is the loss of power they currently wield over young men, particularly, in the areas of marriage, bridewealth, peonage and traditional planting practices. The knowledge of planting season accounts for the traditional hegemony of the elders at the clan level.

II. Marriage System and Bridewealth

In some parts of Igboland, especially the Igbos in the Riverine area of Okrika and Port Harcourt, the marriage institution is very flexible. The bride price is the cornerstone of marital union for the Igbo people. The bride price or bridewealth is the money and goods young men bring to the family of their prospective brides. Tradition allows two types of union between a young man and a woman. The most common forms of marriage among the Ijaws and Ikwere Igbos are the Igwe and Igwu. In Igwe marriage, or concubinage, the union between the man and the woman is not formalized. Igwe is only recognized as a small dowry marriage in which the man only pays a portion of the bridewealth to the father of the bride. This allows for a partial cohabitation between the man and the woman in the house of the parents of the bride. All children born under this union belong to the father of the bride. The father of the bride has the right to put the offspring of the union to work on his personal plot.

As it turns out, many rich members of the clan prefer their daughters to be engaged in the small dowry marriage because it allows them to expand the amount of labour available for use on family plots. Whereas, the poor members of the clan prefer the big dowry (Igwu), since bride price from such union could be used in expanding family plots, or used in setting up shops in the village . For the poor peasants, the big dowry is a means of escaping from village poverty, and improving their social and economic standing in the community.

In the Igwu marriage also known as the big-dowry marriage, the prospective suitors pay a hefty amount of money to the family of the bride, and perform all other ceremonies prescribed by the village elders. Once these are performed, the groom is allowed to take the bride to his own clan. All children born under this relationship belong to the husband, and as a result, increases his social and economic standing in the community. The bride can no longer return to her own clan even when she dies, her remains have to be buried in her husband's house. In the course of this research, it was noticed that this institution of marriage has been greatly affected by the project. The fact that many women can now work outside of the family allows for a greater degree of independence for many peasant women. While older parents continue to arrange marriages for their children, we found that the average age of women entering into any of these marital forms has increased from 14 to 20 years in the short period of time the projects were established. However, the degree to which parents can pressure their eligible children into marriage had diminished significantly. Whereas in Aluu, our control village, we found that many young women are still being forced into early marriage due to economic pressure on the part of their family.

In Ubima and Elele, the introduction of the project has increased the rate at which young men enter into Igwu marriage (big dowry). Most young men can now get jobs at the Nucleus Estate, and within a short period of time, they can save the money needed to perform the big-dowry ceremonies. In a sense, this is a double contradiction in terms of the impact of the project on the marriage system. On the one hand, it has increased the ability of young men to "purchase" their brides more readily, and as such, strengthening their authority over women. At the same time, however, the project has also enabled young and older women to engage in wage labour outside of the household, thereby lessening the burden of patriarchy. Increasingly, at the project villages, many women are asserting their economic independence by making decisions about their lives without seeking approval of the older male members of the household.

In short, the capitalist enterprise at the main Nucleus Estate has benefited greatly from these changes especially in the area of cheap labour supply for the plantation. To some extent, women and young men have also benefited from the project because of the lessening of patriarchal authority over them by village elders. This is because of the fact that the monetarization of the peasant economy allows the release of previously untapped labour of young men and women for exploitation which allowed them an escape route from patriarchal authority of the village elders .

The same dynamics set in motion by the project also continues to condone sexual practices that are patrilocal. For example, in the past, older members of the peasant family often made young men pay bridewealth in two or three forms. Bride price payment could take the form of unpaid labour on the farm of the family of the bride (widespread before the colonial era), or it could be in the form of goods, and more recently, in money form. More and more families are demanding the bridewealth in money form so that they can spend the money on imported goods such as television sets, radios, video equipments and other foreign items imported into the village.

In Aluu village, few changes are taking place with regards to the institution of marriage. Indeed, we encountered a lot of women who are still married under the Igwe system. These women are turned into reproductive machines by their fathers in an effort to increase farm hands on the family plots. On average, a typical Aluu woman has about eight children during her reproductive life. Similarly, patriarchy is still a force to be reckoned with since the households in the Aluu sample are still provided for by a male member. Few women in our Aluu sample work outside of the households, nor partake in the money economy. Those that worked outside of the households, did so on the family plots for subsistence farming.

III. Collective Work Spirit or Communal Work Ethos

Communal work among African peasants is not only extended to agricultural work but also to other areas of social relations. Interaction between the clan community and its physical environment is a collective endeavour while the appropriation of nature resulting from such an endeavour is collectively distributed. Amongst the Ikwere Igbos, such activities as building a house, constructing a bridge and harvesting family plots are generally done collectively. Each member of the clan has the social responsibility of partaking in all of these activities which usually involve unpaid labour. This is often seen as a social debt to the community, and participation in this social work is a restatement of the clan members' commitment to the social contract.

However, the main institutions upon which the communal ethos were founded are crumbling fast in the project villages and adjoining communities. For instance, the dispersal of labour in Ubima and Elele, and the increasing focus on capitalistic reproduction of the clan, meant that very few men and women are available for the age long tradition of communal work. Besides the emergence of petty contractors amongst the rank and file of the peasantry, it also facilitated the decline of cooperative efforts. Similarly, the practice of cooperative savings and lending (esusu) is also fast disappearing. In the past, clan members relied on these communal funds in cases of personal or household emergencies. These communal funds are usually in the form of surplus cash contributed to the village thrift fund, or surplus produce of individual family units which are made available to the entire clan during the off season period. This latter often serves as a source of social security for clan members especially the old, the destitute, and women returning to the clan after the loss of their husbands. This cooperative lending, together with the system of clan support in times of emergency or family disaster, have now been replaced by village money lenders charging exorbitant interest, or by state run agricultural banks which organize monetary relations among the peasantry. It is no coincidence that most of these banks are located in areas which have adopted the integrated agricultural projects.

In the project villages, we found evidence to support a lessening, if not a total demise of communal spirit. The intensification of commodity production, and the speedy moneterization of the peasant economy, had led to social relations being increasingly mediated by market forces. This market induced change has also been accompanied by social problems which are normally associated with city life. At Ubima and Elele, incidents of prostitution among underage girls have multiplied from its pre-project level. In some cases pre-project prostitution in these peasant communities were unheard off. With increasing monetarization of the economy, young women are prostituting themselves to earn cash which they need to purchase foreign commodities that are being gradually introduced into the community.

During a visit to the local police station, this author was told by the police chief that incidents of rape, murder and armed robbery have shot up in the past 10 years since the projects were introduced to the community. These perhaps may be said to be the inevitable negative side effects which modernization has brought to these communities. It is therefore no wonder that at Aluu village where such incidents are still relatively low, and in some villages where such incidents are unheard off, the programme become less attractive.

In fact, most people interviewed in the control village cited rising crime rates and violent disruption in social relations in the project area as the major reasons for resisting the ADPs' experiment in their community. Whether Aluu is able to resist this incursion, especially in the face of the state government's stepped up campaign for a statewide adoption of ADPs remains to be seen. But with the increasing propaganda surrounding the programme, and the need for the state government to increase revenue from export crops and locally produced farm products, it is doubtful whether the village of Aluu will remain untouched.

IV. Class Differentiation

One of the most profound effects of the project is the increasing class differentiation in the project communities. During colonial times, the process of class formation in rural areas was rather slow, and in some cases, existing differences were simply reinforced. Evidence of class differentiation was rather scanty as colonial powers stayed away from disrupting traditional social structure upon which social reproduction was based. Colonial agricultural policy focused on the use of peasants' small unit farms in producing export crops. This practice has been responsible for limiting the emergence of class differences, and hierarchy of exploitative relations that usually characterize large scale commercial agriculture.

Whereas in East Africa, where there is a significant settler population, large scale agricultural plantations are the norms. In the case of settler economies of East Africa, such plantations accelerated the process of class differentiation. Indeed, up to the time of independence in 1960, rural communities in eastern Nigeria were relatively homogeneous. However, since the introduction of the ADPs, differential rate of rural accumulation has facilitated the process of class differentiation resulting in landlessness amongst poor peasants. The principal objective of the ADPs, as stated in the World Bank's guidelines, is to create a stratum of progressive peasant farmers who will adopt all the characteristics of a capitalist farmer. The extension service officers deliberately used the delivery system to create this stratum of progressive farmers. It is important to note, as we pointed out repeatedly in the opening chapters of this work, that before the projects were introduced, land was communally owned.

The concept of private ownership in land was one that accompanied the implementation of the programme. Peasant farmers who do not qualify to join the programme either sell their land or such lands are forcibly taken over by the project's administrator. The rate of landlessness has been going up since the programme was introduced. This trend is causing older members of the clan a lot of concern since they saw land alienation as a threat to the stability of the clan. Indeed as we reported earlier on, younger men alienated from the land are most likely to resort to criminal activities such as armed robbery and petty thievery.

The following tables show the increasing disparity in land ownership among the peasantry with upper and middle peasants controlling more and more land both in the cooperatives and in the smallholders' mini-estates. This is also accompanied by severe landlessness amongst the lowest strata of the peasantry.

**Table 7.2: Peasants' Land Ownership
in the Cooperatives, Block A - Ubima**
Households Ownership %

	(land/ha.)	
2	16	64
4	6	24
19	3	12
25	25	100

N= 25

Source: Compiled from RISADEP's documents,
Port Harcourt, 1991.

**Table 7.3: Peasants' Land Ownership
in the Cooperatives, Block B, Elele-Ahoada**
Households Ownership %

	(land/ha.)	
2	14	56
4	6	24
19	5	20
25	25	100

N=25

Source: Compiled from RISADEP's documents,
Port Harcourt, 1991.

Table 7.4: Peasants' Land Ownership by
Sub-extension Area (Ubima/Elele/Ahoada)
Households Land Ownership   %

	(ha. donated)	
4	30	60
8	12	24
38	8	16
50	50	100

N=50

Table 7.5: Household's Labour
Use per Size of Farm Holdings
Farm Size Permanent Seasonal

(ha.)	labourer	labourer
<.5	0	0
>.5	0	2
1-2.00	2	6
2-5.00	5	12
5-10>	15	20

Source: Fieldwork data 1991.

Initially, the progressive farmers were referred to as contact farmers. These are generally rich peasant farmers. They have in their use, on average, farm sizes of between five to 10 hectares and they routinely use both wage and seasonal labourers on their plots. The extension workers use their farms to test out new technologies before introducing them to the rest of the peasant farmers participating in the programme. As a result of this, the contact farmers receive preferential treatment when it comes to the distribution of fertilizers and the use of heavy duty tractors provided by project's administrators. And because of the fact that these "elite" farmers have the best facilities at their disposal, the productivity on their farms are generally higher than those on the farms of other peasants.

The so-called progressive farmers accumulate faster than other peasants in the two communities studied. They also receive preferential treatment when borrowing money from the rural agricultural banks since they usually have the collateral that is demanded by bank officials. Besides, the progressive farmers, more than any category of peasants, often receive favourable credit ratings from the project officials constituted in the Credit Review Committee (CRC).

The middle peasantry also have access to some of the facilities at the disposal of the project's extension and management office but not to the degree that the progressive farmers do. In fact, both the progressive farmers and the middle peasantry sit on the village advisory committee set up by the management's office to advise the block supervisors on which farmers to admit into the project. The least economically and politically powerful category of the peasants are the lower peasantry and peasant women displaced from their land through land acquisition by the project administrators. The progressive farmers are the major political force, and they are also the main beneficiaries at the village level.

In sum, it is very clear that the World Bank's project has made, and continues to make tremendous impact on these normally sleepy communities. In the concluding chapter, we examine possible alternative development models for Third World agriculture as alternatives to the ones being offered by the World Bank. The concluding chapter also looks at ways in which the current World Bank's agricultural experiment in the developing world can be made to achieve a much more positive result; in order words, producing outcomes that truly benefit the peasant producers.

8 Conclusion

Before this fieldwork was undertaken, my main hypothesis was that capitalist penetration into the rural areas of the Third World would more than likely result in the partial disruption of pre-capitalist modes of production. This was based on the assumption that the penetration of the capitalist mode of production would entail enforcing a partial subsumption of labour, and preserving various pre-capitalist modes to the extent that it will serve the interest of global capital. This partial subsumption of labour, and the strengthening of existing relations within the pre-capitalist modes, the modes of production school argues, will enable capital to reproduce itself.

This theoretical position was vigorously pushed by modes of production scholars like Taylor, (1976), Wolpe (1975), and Laclau (1974). In the early seventies, the modes of production approach came to be accepted, in radical development circles, as a much better theoretical tool than that of the dependency and world system theories for understanding the persistence of crisis of development in the Third World. Indeed, the modes of production theoretical paradigm, as pointed out previously was proposed as a replacement for the dependency and the world system theories that dominated development discourse in the sixties and early seventies. Taylor, in particular, was the most ardent critique of dependency theory, and the most theoretically consistent of all the modes of production scholars.

In *Modernization to Modes of Production*, Taylor (1976) suggests that capitalist penetration of non-capitalist sectors of the Third World only reinforces existing social and economic relations; a situation that capitalism exploits in a continuous search for conditions and avenues for reproducing capital on a global scale. By and large, the articulation of various pre-capitalist modes with the dominant global capitalist system, Taylor contends, sets the conditions for the

114

extended reproduction of capital which ultimately results in the uneven pattern of development that characterize the global economy. According to Taylor, the continuing accumulation of capital, which is a pre-condition for capitalist production, are met by capital's constant search for non-capitalist sectors within the world system for incorporation.

The body of data collected in the course of this research is critical of this conclusion. While capital continuously searches for non-capitalist sectors for accumulation and self reproduction, it does this not by keeping these formations backward or preserving their modes of production, as Taylor and other modes of production theorists suggest, but by encouraging a speedy transformation of these formations along capitalist lines. By extending capitalist relations of production, (for example, capitalization of peasant agriculture, linking peasant production to the urban economy and the global capitalist market), international capital was able to create the conditions under which the intensification of expropriation of peasants' labour and surplus were made possible. In this regard, the ADPs' emphasis on increasing peasants' productivity through the use of fertilizers, and the emphasis on introduction of widespread commodity production, are both aimed at creating the conditions for the reproduction of capital. However, in the process of doing this, slight improvement in the quality of life of the peasant producers was also achieved. Whether this was the original intention of the programme is very difficult to establish given the data presented in this work.

As this research shows, it is not necessarily foreign capital that impedes the transformation of peasants' economy, it is sometimes the degree of peasants' resistance to capitalist incursion that determines the rate of rural transformation. In areas where the rate of resistance is more intense, the tendency is that the rate and scope of rural transformation will be limited. By understanding peasants' resistance to foreign developers, we may understand why the crisis of rural transformation persists in these formations.

Indeed, explaining underdevelopment by reference to the deliberate action and design of global capital, as the dependency and modes of production scholars imply, is nothing short of an explanation by conspiracy. The assumptions of the world system and modes of production theorists are not entirely supported by an examination of the prevailing processes in the Third World. What this research uncovered is that the co-existence between the old and new modes of production (partial subsumption of labour) created the conditions of poverty, which in turn continues to impede the sort of social and economic transformation that capital envisaged for its own good. The peasants' resistance to penetration of capital must be understood from an historically rooted perspective.

The penetration of colonial capital at the turn of the 19th century, and the exploitation of peasants' labour surplus and produce through direct European plunder and pillage, had left the peasants with memories and psyches that are continuously dominated by suspicion of foreign developers. This peculiar attitude of peasants to foreign developers was borne out of peasants' experience of more than one hundred years of European colonialism. It was an experience, some scholars have suggested, that left memories of untold squalor, disease, hunger and gross economic dislocation in the countryside, and of a somewhat deformed capitalist economy in the urban centres (Bigman, 1993).

The current involvement of the World Bank and the International Monetary Fund, in the form of the ADPs, and direct lending for specific development projects in the Third World, should also be seen in the context of the deteriorating global capitalist economy. Since the early seventies, the world economy has been undergoing serious structural crises; crises which directly affects capital reproduction and the process of accumulation. In particular, the commodity crisis of the mid-seventies, which is a consequence of decaying rural production in the Third World, created a challenge to the international capitalist system of production and expropriation.

In addition, the serious imbalance which resulted from the massive movement of capital from the south to the north, as a result of unfair commodity pricing, debt servicing, and unregulated profits transfer by multinational corporations operating in the Third World, had led to a serious crisis in these formations (Susan, 1992). It is thus the opinion of this author that this crisis directly posed a serious problem for the global capitalist economy, and therefore, redressing this crisis in the South became the pre-occupation of global capital. It is within this theoretical assumption that we choose to understand the current World Bank involvement in Third World development process. The main concern then is to examine how adequately World Bank's policies of integrated rural development and structural adjustment are explained by this paradigm. This work, therefore, suggests that externally imposed development projects often produce unexpected effects. While development assistance have the potential of reinforcing the condition of external dependence, and thereby creating new obstacles that may impede the development process, it also may produce consequences other than dependence. There are certainly some contradictory tendencies, with respect to some aspects of ADPs, as the findings of this research show.

In the case of the ADPs examined for this study, while the projects succeeded in extending capitalist relations of production within the peasant mode of production, and in the process increased the productivity of peasant producers, nevertheless their most significant achievement was in reinforcing peasants' dependence on the external global system of capitalist production. The emphasis of the projects on export crop production, and the dependence on externally developed technology, further facilitated the integration of the peasants' economy to the world economic system. This process of integration has the potential of further restricting, unless emphasis is placed on internally generated resources and technology, the possibility of independent and sustained development of the national economy.

However, this conclusion should be seen and situated within the theoretical perspective informed by the political economy approach. While Karl Marx might be correct in his comments on the expansionary character of capital into non-capitalist formations for purposes of capital's reproduction, he was, however slightly off course in suggesting that such penetration will result in capitalism recreating those formations in its own image (Marx, 1971). The penetration of capitalist mode of production into Third World formations, in the past hundred or so years, was one that resulted not in the development of capitalism proper, but in the development of a disoriented system of production that was neither capitalist nor feudal. The present Nigerian economic model exemplifies clearly the problems engendered by this sort of neo-colonial transformation.

In *Imperialism, Pioneer of Capitalism*, Warren (1979) criticizes neo-Marxists scholars for ignoring the sort of capitalist development taking place in the Third World. He argues that the level of industrialization that had been achieved by this penetration of Third World formations was significant enough to be ignored. Warren notes, however, that neo-Marxist scholars sometimes confuse capitalist industrialization with the general advance in the standard of living and improvement in social conditions for the underclass. Warren contends that even in the advanced capitalist countries, improvement in social and economic conditions of subordinate classes, was hardly the goal of capitalist development.

This conclusion by Warren was drawn from a particular reading of Marx's original texts in Capital and the Critique of Political Economy, in which Marx contends that capitalism as a mode of production, with all its revolutionary possibilities, is incapable of resolving fundamental problems of poverty and social inequities. This is because these are the pre-requisites for class domination upon which capitalism is founded.

If we can borrow a leaf from Warren's ideas, it could be argued, as I tried to do in this work, that capitalist sponsored development efforts in the Third World are not intended solely to improve the quality of life in these formations, nor are they intended to promote an agenda of social and economic equity as some Third World scholars often expected. The developmental efforts, on the part of the World Bank and other capitalist institutions, are in large part geared primarily towards extending capitalist relations of production in the peripheral formations of the World economy. It is thus argued here that capital's penetration of pre-capitalist formations often unconsciously reinforce existing inequalities by creating new social structures that make exploitation of these formations possible. This process is dictated by capital's rational search for profit. Nevertheless, this same process may also lead to increasing peasants' productivity, most especially in export related activities, as this research has shown. Moreover, there is ample evidence to affirm that the ADPs have served as an agent of change in the communities studied. This is most significantly demonstrated in the process of class differentiation that has taken place, and also in the challenge to the political authority of the elders, in the communities where the projects were located.

Capitalism and Social Classes

The process of class differentiation, and the on-going agrarian accumulation in rural Nigeria, clearly support the contention that the projects have the tendency of extending class relations in the countryside. To expect capitalism to transform social and economic relations in the Third World in the direction that will make capital accumulation impossible will run counter to the logic of global capital accumulation essential for the maintenance of the system of regional inequality created by capitalism. And this is what the politics of development is all about.

This is, indeed, the contention of the modes of production school, and supported by the arguments propounded throughout this work. But the point of departure between my findings and the modes of production position is that the same process that made capital accumulation possible also encouraged increasing peasants' productivity. More importantly, the inability of the modes of production scholars to realize that the interest of capital, and by some irony of fate, the interest of certain ranks of peasant farmers, are best served by extending the process of capitalist relations to pre-capitalist structures is perhaps one of the many drawbacks of their analysis.

However, the modes of production and other Marxists scholars are correct in claiming that capitalism, as a destructive mode of production, relies and survives on the maintenance of social inequality between classes, and especially, the maintenance of absolute poverty by excluding the lower classes from owning the means of self reproduction. This exclusion of producers from the means of production allows for accumulation by a tiny urban elite at the national level. On the international level, this relation is reproduced by global capital, through the concentration of accumulation in the hands of metropolitan elites. The tiny bourgeoisie in the underdeveloped section of the World economy only serve as conduits through which the economic aspirations of international capital are realized.

In *How Europe Underdeveloped Africa*, Walter Rodney concludes that the European economic hegemony, which was made possible by the acquisition of colonial properties by the metropolitan elites, was perhaps the most decisive factor in the unequal relations between the developed North and the least developed countries in the South. In other words, the same process of colonialism which made European capitalist hegemony possible also led to the stagnation of the economies of the African states. Indeed, capitalist accumulation and reproduction globally continue to be sustained by a constant search for sectors of the global economy where conditions are much more favourable. These conditions may be in the form of cheap labour, or in the form of new investment possibilities.

Capitalism, Imperialism and Modern Colonies

It has been proposed by Marxist scholars that capitalist imperialism needs colonies for its reproduction. First, it needs expanded market for its reproduction, a market which the colonies provided. Second, it also needs cheap resources so that capitalist profit could be attained without having to keep wages down or below what is required for their reproduction. As Stavenhagen (1973) observes, these two conditions are no longer present and available in the case of late capitalist development. As a result, the process of capitalist transformation becomes an uphill battle for the majority of the developing societies who are caught up in the quagmire and painful realities of capitalist underdevelopment.

If we accept these arguments, then we can begin to question the validity of the liberal development position that sees external investment as the only solution to Third World development crisis. It could also be argued that since the main development paradigms that have informed development planning in most

119

of these formations were the Rostowrian and neo-Rostowrian perspectives, their persistent failure simply calls to question the plausibility of the modernization models, whether in Third World agriculture or industry. For instance, multinationals' investment decisions abroad are motivated by a rational search for profit, as a result, those multinational corporations constantly explore regions within the world economy that provide the highest returns on their investment. Neo-Marxist analyses of the expansion of capital to the developing World often ignore this essential need for capital to be rational in its behaviour, otherwise reproducing capital on the global scale will not be possible. This is indeed one of the shortfalls of the dependency's theoretical analysis of the problems of underdevelopment in the Third World. It is within this context of capital's rational search for reproductive conditions that we situate our analysis of the continuing crisis of transformation in the least developed sections of the world economy.

The "new capitalist development" thesis that is being advanced to explain the on-going dependent development in certain sections of the periphery (South Korea, Taiwan, Thailand and Hong Kong), misunderstood the modes of production school's position with regards to the peculiar nature of this late capitalist development. Evans, for example, is among those scholars who are speaking of the "economic miracles" that are currently taking place in these so called "new capitalist zones" of the world system. What is often lost in this debate is that, despite increasing industrialization in these new capitalist zones of the world economy, the process simply demonstrates the need for international capital to allow for new centres of dependent capitalist development, in the face of an increasing threat to capital from both internal social classes in the new capitalist zones, and the intensification of the cold war which aimed at curtailing the spread of communism.

The point that is being made here is that by promoting capitalist development, particularly in the most sensitive sections of the world system, capitalist hegemonic states could defend themselves more effectively from the perceived threat of Soviet and Chinese communism. Indeed, the "alliance for progress ideology" put forward by the West is a good illustration of this point. This is one way of saying that we can hardly separate this late capitalist development from the politics and ideology of the cold war. But whether the end of the cold war will change this remains to be seen. However, this is not to suggest that the process of sustained development in the Third World is not possible. What is being suggested is that the capitalist road to social and economic transformation in the developing societies has a lot of obstacles to overcome given the various reasons we outlined above.

While it is true that the World Bank's assistance in the form of the projects we studied in the course of this research, has contributed to the process of economic transformation in the communities we studied, however, it has not entirely succeeded in achieving the goals of establishing the foundation for a sustainable, and internally generated development. If the ADPs' goals were to be achieved, the process has to be taken over by the developing states. In other words, the inputs delivery system, and technology application (i.e., defining appropriate technology), have to be decided by local officials in collaboration with the more knowledgeable stratum of the peasantry. By sitting in meetings where decisions are made, middle and upper strata of the peasantry are increasingly coopted into the overall agenda of the programme, which is commercial crop production.

What is the Way Forward?

The acceptance of the capitalist road to economic transformation in agriculture and industry by African states has allowed the penetration of neo-colonial capital with stifling consequences. The African neo-colonial states' collaboration with international capital has provided the basis for the persistent failure of transformation. The dominance of neo-colonial capital continues to preclude the possibility of a realistic alternative to this crisis.

In Nigeria, the neo-colonial state persists in collaborating with international capital, and as a result, exacerbates the economic crisis. The crisis precipitated by this collaboration necessitated the type of assistance sought from the World Bank in the form of the ADPs. The apparent difficulties encountered by the ADPs in resolving the problems of rural poverty, even when it has succeeded in improving peasants' productivity in export created activities, call into question the relevance of this capitalist model in Third World agriculture. The difficulty encountered by the programme, in establishing a permanent structure for sustainable and viable agricultural growth, may be due partly to the hierarchical structure of the ADPs. But this could be resolved, if the project administrators involve the peasant producers more in the planning and execution stages of the projects.

Given the commitment of the Nigerian state to the capitalist road to economic development, one way the ADPs could work is through the intervention of the state. The Nigerian state should insist on popular participation in the design, execution and the administration of the projects. Since this popular participation may conflict with the interest of international finance institutions providing funding for the projects, the solution will be for the Nigerian state to take over the funding, and scale down the budget of the ADPs so that resources could be generated internally to finance its own development. An internal consensus can be built regarding decisions about what is to be produced, how it is produced, and the appropriate methods of production. This process should involve the peasant producers themselves. The constant switch of family plots by peasants to the production of food crops rather than to export crops that the project administrators demanded, exemplifies the difficulties inherent in projects in which decision making process is from top down as opposed to bottom up.

The other difficulty relates to the type of technology that is currently prescribed to improve peasants' productivity. The emphasis of management on the production of export crops has led to the application of high technology, foreign inputs, and a management style that runs against traditional peasants' attitudes. In an effort to increase peasants' productivity, this author does not believe that undue emphasis should be placed on replicating high technology that has been proven to work well in the advanced economy of the West. All technologies are culturally specific, and this cultural specificity determines the success or failure of their application. If the ADPs are to succeed, emphasis should be placed on the development of intermediate technology or appropriate technology, one that could be developed in collaboration with the peasant producers themselves.

This is where the question of culturally specific research becomes of crucial importance. The experience in Nigeria, and indeed other neo-colonial states in Africa, has been an over reliance on externally developed technology that was based on social and cultural conditions of peoples elsewhere. In order to break the problem of technological dependence, African states should consider and adopt those development aid packages that are relevant to their particular needs. In addition, these states should also strive for innovation in engineering, science and management. However, this could only be achieved by a radical restructuring of the education institutions to make them more relevant to the African conditions.

As it is now, African engineers and other professionals are still being trained in western metropolitan institutions where they continue to be knowledgeable in foreign ideas and ignorant of their own physical environment. Therefore, making research and science relevant to the African experience, and digging back to the abundant technological experience of the African past may be the only solution to the question of African backwardness and dependence. And of course, all of these depend on the degree to which international capital will cooperate in relieving African states of their chains of dependence. Indeed, the picture looks rather gloomy in the face of the current direction of the world economy and the collapse of Soviet communism. Essentially, the collapse of pockets of ideological alternatives to western imperialism means an increasing expansion of capitalist mode of production into areas that are previously socialist. More so, the new world order, which may not take the interests and concerns of Third World states seriously, may further hamper the process of economic transformation in these formations.

This unfolding scenario, in the global economy, leaves Africa with a big question mark. Nonetheless, despite the pessimistic picture of economic transformation drawn in this concluding part, there are still some possibilities for the future. It is doubtful that the international community will show any serious interest in the question of Africa's economic recovery since global resources are being increasingly diverted to the former socialist states in an effort to initiate some sort of late capitalist development in these newly incorporated regions of the world capitalist economy. However, Africa has the capacity both in human and mineral resources, and with the development of a democratic order, she will eventually surmount her current crisis. The future, indeed, is the African peasant producers.

Postscript

Since writing up this research report, the World Bank has announced a drastic change in the way it approaches its integrated rural development programme. It is very important to examine this change in strategy and see how it will affect development process in the developing world. In its latest publication *The World Bank Participation Source Book (1996)*, the bank fell short of admitting failure of its agricultural policies towards the developing world. In the early seventies, as we outlined in the preceding chapters, the World Bank popularized Integrated Rural Development Programme (IRDP) as a means of boosting productivity of peasant farmers in Africa and southeast Asia by emphasizing a capitalist transformation of agriculture.

Up to the nineties, in spite of glaring failure of this approach, the bank insisted that this programme provided the best solution to the problems of famine, and crop failures in most of the non-industrial world. The reasoning behind this claim is in the three fundamental assumptions of the rural integrated programme. These assumptions are: a) a belief that the introduction of high yielding hybrid crops would boost peasants productivity, b) that the use of fertilizers and the provision of extension advice by extension officers would break peasants' traditional practices; and c) that creating a category of capitalist farmers would automatically result in widespread rural transformation. And for years the bank relied on expert advice and ignored the wisdom of the poor farmers they were trying to help.

The result of this approach, as we argued in the body of this work, is that many of these economies were either destroyed, disrupted or forced into desperation because of the bank's emphasis on export related production. It is thus not a dubious exercise that the IRDP and ADP have been criticized for decades by scholars who believed that these programmes, like the present structural adjustment programme (SAP), simply strengthened the historical link of dependence between the developing nations and the western industrial economies. Indeed, independent researchers have documented, as is obvious in this research, how the bank's projects have impoverished farmers worldwide by the deliberate creation of poverty and famine in much of the developing world (see Christofersson, 1980). Why it took the World Bank this long to realize the absurdity of its agricultural programs in sub-Saharan Africa and Asia, where millions have perished in hunger, is certainly beyond comprehension. However, the bank should also be commended for being bold enough to admit its failure, and let us hope that its latest approach, as contained in the book, provides directions in terms of ingredients that correct the mistakes of the past.

Unfortunately, *The World Bank Participation Source Book* is directed towards development experts, and not the poor peasants it hopes to help. Because of its highly technical language, it is extremely doubtful whether this book would lead to a genuine agrarian reform in the developing world, at least in the short term. For instance the bank's strong recommendation of popular participation in production without a corresponding participation in the polity, and the decision making process within the world economy, sounds rather naive. It sounds rather like a hollow prescription for the many poor folks in this increasingly polarized world economy.

The general idea in the book is that the bank can provide better extension services to poor farmers in the developing world by listening to them, and by letting them have a major control in the administration of her funded projects.

This will include decisions relating to what they produce, how they produce and what method they adopt in production without the bank's officials getting in the way. This "bottom-up" approach is a significant and radical departure from the old model where extension officers and bank's officials, who lack knowledge of local people, their cultures, language and value system were at the centre of production.

The book itself is a self serving collaborative work by the bank's experts and economists who have direct contact with agricultural development projects in the developing world. In all, it contains 16 case studies of the bank's funded agricultural development projects in countries as far and remote as Albania, Brazil, India, Lao, Nigeria, and Yemen. In addition to the case studies, there are 12 technical papers dealing with specific subjects such as the role of participation in production, poverty assessments, education and training programmes, gender issue in production, and the role of non-governmental organizations (NGOs) in the development process. The overall goal of the book, as spelled out in the foreword by the bank's president, is to hand over the development process to the people.

This is definitely a very technical book that will be found useful and handy by policy makers in the developing world where participatory approach in agricultural production can provide the answer to the age long problems of crop failures and famine. However, it is certainly not an appropriate book for poor farmers who can barely read or write. The audience would probably be development agencies and donor nations around the world who will, hopefully, find the book a useful instrument in the development process. In this regard, the book is a good addition to existing work in this area. The ideas contained in the book are not novel, but what distinguishes it from the others is its wealth of technical data and instruments which previously have not been made available to researchers.

While the bank's officials now concede to the failure of the past, it is very difficult at this time to evaluate the merits of this new approach given the prevailing economic conditions in most of the developing world. One crucial impediment to the execution of this new approach will be the continuing implementation of the policy of structural adjustment (SAP), which so far, has contributed to the destruction of many Third World economies particularly in Africa and Latin America. The policy of structural adjustment, over the past ten years or so, has only intensified both rural and urban poverty, disease, famine, political instability, political repression, and a complete destruction of civil societies in Africa, and in much of the developing world.

As someone who is very familiar with the bank's projects in Africa, it is very difficulty for me to accept this new strategy given the bank's lack of genuine commitment to development and regional stability in the least developed section of the global economy. If the new "bottom up" approach is to work, the bank, and the IMF must relent on their current aggressive policies of adjustment. For instance, what my field data revealed, as documented in the body of this work, is that while farmers' productivity actually rose, it did so mainly in export related activities, and without a corresponding rise in food production. The bank's idea that farmers could make money growing export crops, and then use income deriving from such activity to purchase imported or very expensive locally produced food, is not only absurd but illogical. For example, when I revisited the projects in the summer of this year, I found that the gains in farmers' productivity have further been wiped out by currency devaluation, which is a major requirement under the structural adjustment programme. It is thus difficult to see how participatory approach in agriculture is going to produce a tangible result when the rest of the economy is running triple digit inflation caused by the implementation of the structural adjustment programme.

It is against this background that this author doubts very much how this new latest approach is going to contribute to the promotion of a viable and internally generated growth. As of now, the bank has a very bad, and poor record in the developing countries, and I certainly do not see how this record is going to be corrected by their book, contrary to the optimism expressed by the bank's president.

Finally the next decade will probably be a test point for the World Bank in terms of the role it has taken upon itself as the development agent. Given the current social and political direction in many African countries most especially the spread of dictatorial, and patrimonial regimes everywhere, and with the connivance of metropolitan powers with African dictators, it is most unlikely that Africa will recover from the burden of European domination anytime soon. It has been shown that the main pre-condition for economic development is political stability, but with the interventionist roles of First World multinational corporations in forestalling democratic transitions in most development countries, the bank's commitment to economic development in the Third World will probably remain the subject of the 21st century.

Bibliography

Abdullahi, Y. A. 1982. "The state and agrarian crisis in Nigeria: rhetoric and substance of Nigerian Agricultural development, paper presented at Workshop on State of the Nigerian Economy, ABU: 19-21 October, 1983.

Adams, P. 1992. "The World Bank and the IMF in Sub-Saharan Africa: Undermining Development and Sustainability." *Journal of International Affairs*, Summer 1992, 46, no. 1, pp.97-116.

Adedeji, A. 1969. "Federalism, Economic Planning and Plan Administration." *NISER Conference Paper*.

_____ 1989. *Towards a Dynamic African Economy*, London, Zed Press.

Afigbo, A.E. 1972. *The warrant chiefs: Indirect rule in southeastern Nigeria 1891 - 1929*. London: Longman.

Ake, C. 1985. *The Political Economy of Nigeria, London and Nigeria*, Longman Press.

Akeredolu, E. 1975. The Underdevelopment of Indigenous Entrepreneurship in Nigeria. Ibadan: University Press.

Anikpo, M. 1985. "Mobilizing the Peasantry for National Resistance." in G.O. Nwabueze (ed.) *Mass Mobilization and National Self-Reliance*. Port-Harcourt: Faculty of Social Sciences, University of Port Harcourt, Mimeo.

127

Bibliography

Alavi, H. 1972. "The Post-Colonial State." *London: New Left Review*, 74, July-August. pp.59-82.

Amin, S. 1974. *Imperialism and Unequal Development*. New York: Monthly Review Press.

_____ 1974. *Accumulation on a World Scale*. Monthly Review Press.

_____ 1976 *Unequal Development: An Essay on the Formation of Peripheral Capitalism*. New York: Monthly Review Press.

Aribisala, T.S. 1983. *Nigerian's Green Revolution: Achievements, Problems and Prospects*. Ibadan: Niser Mimeograph series.

Arrighi, G. 1978. "Towards a Theory of Capitalist Crisis." *New Left Review*, no.111 pp.3-24

_____ 1982. *The Geometry of Imperialism*. London: Verso Books.

_____ 1982. "A Crisis of Hegemony," in Samir Amin et al. (eds.) *Dynamics of Global Crisis*. New York: Monthly Review Press.

Auer, P., (ed.), 1981. *Energy and the Developing Nations*. New York: Pergamon Press.

Ayres, R.C. 1983. *Banking on the Poor*. Cambridge, Mass: MIT Press.

Babai, Don. 1993. "The World Bank," in Joel Krieger, (ed.), *The Oxford Companion to World Politics*. Oxford: Oxford University Press.

Badru, P. 1982. "Aspects of Rural Transformation in the Sociology of Development: The Role of the Military in Land Reform in Nigeria". *Unpublished Msc.dissertation*, London School of Economics, London, England.

_____ 1984. "Oil Revenue and the Rural-Urban Dichotomy in Nigerian Development Experience." *Journal of African Urban Studies*.

_____ 1987. "Marital Forms Among the Ijaw People of South Eastern Nigeria". Atlanta: *Heritage Magazine, Issue No.*1, pp.25-27

Baran, P. 1952. *On the Political Economy and Backwardness.* Manchester School of Economic and Social Studies, 20:66-84.

Barker, J. (ed.), 1984. *The Politics of Agriculture in Africa.* London: Sage Publications.

Bates, R. 1974. *Pattern of Uneven Development: Causes and Consequences in Zambia.* Denver: University of Denver Press.

____ 1981. *Markets and State in Tropical Africa.* Berkeley, University of California Press.

Beckman, B. 1982. "Whose State? State and Capitalist Development in Nigeria," *Review of African Political Economy (ROAPE)*, 10: 60-73.

_____ 1985. "Bakolori: peasants versus the state and capital." *Nigerian Journal of Political Science,* Vol.4 (1-2), pp.76-104.

Beneria, Lourdes, and Gita Sen. "Accumulation, reproduction and women's role in economic development: Boserup revisited." *Signs*, vol. 7, no. 2 (winter 1981): 279-298.

_____ and Shelley Feldman, (eds.), *Unequal burden: economic crises, persistent poverty, and women's work.* Boulder: Westview Press, 1992.

Berg, E. 1981. *Accelerated Development in Sub-Saharan Africa: An Agenda for Action.* Washington, D.C: World Bank.

Bernstein, H. 1976. "African Peasantries: A Theoretical Framework." *Journal of Peasant Studies*, vol. 6, No. 4, pp.421-443.

Bigman, L. 1993. *History and Hunger in West Africa.* Westport, Connecticut: Greenwood Press.

129

Block, F. 1977. *The Origins of the International Economic Disorder*. New York: Oxford Press.

Boserup, Esther. 1970. *The role of women in economic development*. New York: St. Martin's Press.

Brett, E.A. 1985. *The World Economy Since the War: The Politics of Uneven Development*. New York: Praeger Books.

Browsberger, W. 1983. "Development and Governmental Corruption in Nigeria: Materialism and Political Fragmentation in Nigeria." *Journal of Modern African Studies*, 21, 2, pp.215-233.

Buestecker, T. 1978. *Distortions or Development: Contending Perspectives on Multinational Corporations*. Massachussetts: MIT Press.

Cardoso, F.H. 1972. *Dependency and Underdevelopment in Latin America*. New York: Random House.

Central Banks of Nigeria. *Annual Reports*. Lagos: Nigeria

Charlton, S.E.M. 1984. *Women in Third World Development*. Boulder, Colorado: Westview Press.

Christie, R. 1980. "Why Does Capital Need Energy?" In T. Turner and P. Nore (eds.), *Oil and Class Struggle*. London: Zed Press.

Chinzea, B. 1985. "The Dialectics of Self-Reliance and Political Order in Nigeria," in G.O. Nwabueze (ed.) *Mass Mobilization and National Self-Reliance*. Port Harcourt: Faculty of Social Sciences, University of Port Harcourt, Mimeo.

Christofferson, L.E. 1980. "The World Bank and Rural Poverty," in *The World Bank and the World's Poorest*. World Bank: Washington, D.C.

Clark, J. 1979. *Agricultural Production in Rural Yoruba Town*. Ph.D. dissertation, University of London.

Clawson, P. 1980. "The Internationalization of Capital and Capital Accumulation in Iran," in T. Turner and P. Nore, (eds.), *Oil and Class Struggle*. London: Zed Press.

Collier, P. 1981. "Oil and Inequality in Rural Nigeria." in *ILO World Employment Paper (Research Working Paper)*.

Dennis, C, 1987, "Women and the State in Nigeria: The Case of the Federal Military Government, 1984-85," in Afshar, H. (ed.), *Women State and Ideology: Studies from Africa and Asia*. Albany: SUNY Press.

Dike, A. 1956. *The Crown Prince of the Niger*. Oxford: Oxford University Press.

Dos Santos, T. 1973 "The Crisis of Development Theory and the Problem of Dependence in Latin America", in H. Bernstein (ed.), *Underdevelopment and Development*. Harmondsworth: Penguin Books.

Dunmoye, R.A. 1982. "The Greening of Capitalist Agriculture in Nigeria, " *Ufahamu*, 12: 123-151.

_____ 1986. "The State and Peasantry: The Politics of Integrated Rural Development Projects in Nigeria." Unpublished Ph.D. dissertation, University of Toronto, Canada.

_____ 1989. "The Political Economy of Agricultural Production in Africa: State Capital and the Peasantry," *Journal of Peasant Studies*, vol. 16, 2, pp.87-104.

ECLA 1990. *Economic Report on Africa, 1990*. United Nations Economic Commission for Africa: Addis Abba, Ethiopia.

Eicher, C.K. and C. Liedholm, (eds.), 1970. *Growth and the Development of Nigerian Economy*. East Lansing: Michigan State University Press.

_____ and D.C. Baker. 1982. *Research on Agricultural Development in Sub-Saharan Africa*. East Lansing: Michigan State University Press.

_____ and Staatz, J.M. 1990. *Agricultural Development in the Third*

World. Baltimore: The Johns Hopkins University Press.

Eisenstadt, N. 1965. *Tradition, Change and Modernity*. Englewood, New Jersey: Prentice-Hall.

_____ 1966. *Modernization, Protest and Change*. New Jersey: Prentice Hall.

Elson, Diane. "How is structural adjustment affecting women?" *Development*, 1 (1989): 67-74.

_____ "From survival strategies to transformation strategies: women's needs and structural adjustment," in Lourdes Beneria and Shelley Feldman, (eds.), *Unequal burden: economic crises, persistent poverty, and women's work*. Boulder: Westview Press, 1992, 26-48.

Emmanuel, A. 1972. *Unequal Exchange and the Imperialism of Trade*. New York: Monthly Review Press.

Evans, P. 1979. *Dependent Development*. Princeton, New Jersey: Princeton University Press.

Falola, T. and Ihonvbere, J. 1985. *The Rise and Fall of Nigeria's Second Republic*. London: Zed Press.

FAO.1976. *Perspective Study on Agricultural Development in the Sahelian Countries, 1975-1990*. 3 Vols, Rome.

Feder, E. 1976. "The New World Bank Program for Self-Liquidation of Third World Peasantry." *Journal of Peasant Studies* 3: 343-54.

Federal Republic of Nigeria,1962. *First National Plan, 1962-1968*. Lagos: Ministry of Finance.

Federal Republic of Nigeria, 1970. *Second National Plan, 1970-1974*. Lagos, Nigeria: Ministry of Finance.

_____ 1975. *Third National Plan, 1975-1980.* Lagos, Nigeria: Ministry of Finance.

_____ 1980. *Fourth National Plan, 1981-85.* Lagos: Ministry of Finance.

Federici, Silvia. 1990. "The debt crisis, Africa and the new enclosures." *Midnight Notes* 10, pp. 10-17.

Fieldhouse, D.H. 1986. *Black Africa, 1945-86; Economic Decolonization and Arrested Development.* London: Allen and Unwin.

Frank, A.G. 1966. "'The Development of Underdevelopment." in *Monthly Review* 18(No.4).

_____ 1967. *Capitalism and Underdevelopment in Latin America.* New York: Monthly Review Press.

_____ 1974. *The Development of Underdevelopment.* New York, Monthly Review Press.

_____ 1980. *Crisis in the Third World.* New York.

Furtado, C. 1965. "Development and Stagnation in Latin America: A Structural Approach." *Studies in Comparative Development,* no.1, 11.

_____ 1970. *Economic Development of Latin America.* Cambridge: Cambridge Press.

_____ 1973. "The Concept of External Dependence in the Study of Underdevelopment," in C.K. Wilber (ed.), *The Political Economy of Development and Underdevelopment.* New York: Random House.

Gallaher, M. 1991. *Rent Seeking and Economic Growth in Africa.* Boulder, Colorado,Westview Press.

George, Susan. 1992. *The debt boomerang: how third world debt harms us all.* Boulder: Westview Press.

Bibliography

Gittinger, J.P.1989. *Economic Analysis of Agricultural Projects*. Baltimore, John Hopkins Univ. Press.

Griffin, K. 1972. *The Green Revolution: An Economic Analysis*. Harmondsworth: Penguin Books.

Gutkind et al. 1976. *The Political Economy of Contemporary Africa*. Beverley Hills, Carlifornia: Sage Press.

Harris, J. 1982. *Rural Development: Theories of Peasant Economy and Agrarian Change*. London: Hutchinson University Press.

Hart, K. 1982. *The Political Economy of West Africa Agriculture*. London: Cambridge University Press.

Helleiner, G. 1966. *Peasant Agriculture, Government, and Economic Growth in Nigeria*. Homewood ILL: R.D. Irwin.

_____ 1986. *Africa and the IMF*. Washington: IMF-publications.

Heyer, J. and G. Williams, (eds.), 1981. *Rural Development in Tropical Africa*. London: Macmillan Press.

Hirschman, A.O. 1958. *The Strategy of Economic Development*. New Haven: Yale University Press.

_____ 1981. *Essays in Trespassing: Economic to Politics and Beyond*. New York: Cambridge University Press.

Hyden, G. 1980. *Beyond Ujamaa: Underdevelopment and the Uncaptured Peasantry*. London: Hienemann.

_____ 1983. *No Shortcut to Progress: African Development Management in Perspective*. Berkeley: University of California Press.

Hutchful, E. 1985. "Texaco Funiwa-5 Oil Blowout, Rivers State, Nigeria." *Journal of African Marxists*, No. 7. pp.51-62.

_____ 1989. *The IMF and Ghana: A Confidential Report.* London: Zed Press.

Ihimodu, I. 1991. "Agricultural Policy," in Ben Turok (ed.), *IFAA Conference Papers on the African Crisis.*

Iyegha, D.A. 1988. *Agricultural Crisis in Africa: The Nigerian Experience. Lanham.* Maryland: University Press of America.

Jorgenson, D.W. 1961. "Development of a Dual Economy." *Economic Journal* 72 (June):309-34.

Kautsky, K. 1889. *The Agrarian Problem.* London: Frank Cass.

Kilby, P. 1945-1966. *Industrialization in an Open Society -Nigeria.*

Koehn, P. 1979. "Ethiopia: Famine, Food Production and Changes in the Legal Order," *African Studies Review,* 22, 1, pp.51-71.

Laclau, E. 1971. "Feudalism and Capitalism in Latin America," *New Left Review,* 67 (May-June 1971). pp.19-38.

_____ 1977. *Politics and Ideology in Marxist Theory of Capitalism.* London, New Left Books.

Lehman, D. (ed.), 1974. *Agrarian Reform and Agrarian Reformism.* London: Faber.

Lele, U. and Agarwal, M. 1989. *Smallholder and Large Scale Agriculture in Africa: Are there Trade Offs Between Growth and Equity.* MADAI Project. Washington, World Bank.

Lenin, V.I. 1966. *Imperialism: The Highest Stage of Capitalism.* New York: Bantam Books.

Lerner, Daniel. *1958. The Passing of Traditional Society.* New York: Free Press.

135

Lewis, A. 1955. "Economic Development With Unlimited Labor Supply." *Manchester School of Economic and Social Studies*, 22(2):139-91.

_____ 1978. *The Evolution of the International Economic Order.* Princeton: Princeton University Press.

Leys, C. 1975. *Underdevelopment in Kenya.* London: Heineman.

Lipton, M. 1976. *Why Poor People Stay Poor: Urban Bias in World Development.* Cambridge. Mass: Harvard University Press.

Manley, M. 1980. "Message to the South-North Conference on the International Monetary System and the New International Order," *Development Dialogue*, no.2, pp.4-6.

Martin, G.W. (ed.) 1990. *Semiperipheral States in the World-Economy.* Westport, Connecticut: Greenwood Press.

Marx, K. 1971. *Capital Vol. I.* International Publishers: New York.

Maurice, D. 1972. Political Economy and Capitalism. Greenwood Press: Greenwich, Connecticut.

McClelland, R. 1977, *The Achieving Society.* Prentice-Hall: New York.

McNamara, R. 1973. *Address to the World Bank's Board of Governors.* Washington, D.C.

Meillassoux, Claude. 1975. *Maids, meals and money: capitalism and the domestic community.* Cambridge: Cambridge University Press, 1986.

Mies, Maria. 1984. "Capitalism and subsistence: rural women in India." *Development* (Journal of the Society for International Development, Rome) 4, pp. 18-25.

_____ 1986. *Patriarchy and accumulation on a world scale: women in the international division of labour.* London: Zed Press.

_____ Claudia von Werlhof and Veronika Bennholdt-Thomsen. 1988. *Women, the last colony.* London: Zed Press.

Mistry, P. 1990. *The Present Role of the World Bank in Africa.* London, IFAA.

Nabudere, D. 1978. *The Political Economy of Imperialism.* London: Zed Press.

Nelson, H.D. 1981. *Nigeria: a Country Study.* Washington: American University's Foreign Area Study.

O'Connor, J. 1984. *Accumulation Crisis.* New York: Basil Blackwell.

Ogba, P.C. 1980. *Operation Feed the Nation in Nigeria.* Ph.D. dissertation, Indiana University.

Olatunbosun, M. 1975. *Nigeria's Neglected Rural Majority.* Ibadan: Oxford University Press.

Olayide, S. 1972. "Agriculture in the federal republic of Nigeria", in O. Oyediran (ed.), *Survey of Nigerian Affairs.*

Onimade, B. 1982. *Imperialism and Underdevelopment.* London: Zed Books.

_____ 1983. *Multinational Corporations in Nigeria.* Ibadan: University Press.

_____ 1983. *Imperialism and Underdevelopment in Nigeria.* London: Zed Press.

_____ 1988. *A Political Economy of the African Crisis.* London: Zed Press.

_____ 1989. *The IMF, World Bank and Africa.* London: IFAA and Zed Press.

_____ 1989. *The IMF, World Bank and the African Debt Crisis.* London: IFAA and Zed Press.

Othman, H. 1990. *Alternative Development Strategy for Africa.* London: IFAA (Institute for Africa Alternatives).

Paige, J. 1975. *Agrarian Revolution: Social Movements and Export Agriculture in the Underdeveloped World.* New York: Macmillan.

Panther-Brick, K., (ed.) 1978. "The Political Transformation of Nigeria." *Soldiers and Oil.* London: Frank Cass.

Payer, C. 1986. *The World Bank: A Critical Analysis.* New York: MRP.

Petras, J. 1978. *Critical Perspectives on Imperialism and Social Class in the Third World.* New York: New Left Books.

Prebisch, R. 1959. "Commercial Policy in the Underdeveloped Countries." *American Economic Review,* 64 (May):251-273.

Piji, K. 1984. *The Making of an Atlantic Ruling Class.* London: Verso Press.

Post, K. 1977. "Peasantization in Western Africa." In P. Gutkind and Watterman, (eds.), *African Social Studies: A Radical Reader.* New York: Monthly Review Press.

Pratt, R.C. 1983. "The Global Impact of the World Bank," in Jill Torrie (ed.), *Banking on Poverty: The Global Impact of the IMF and World Bank.* Toronto: Between the Line Press.

Quijano, A. 1971. *Nationalism and Capitalism in Peru: A Study of Neo-Colonialism.* London: Monthly Review Press

Ranis, G. 1964. *The Development of the Labor Surplus Economy: Theory and Policy.* Homewood, IL: Richard D. Irwin.

Rodney, W. 1972. *How Europe Underdeveloped Africa.* London, Beacon Books.

Rostow, W. 1963. *The Stages of Growth: A non-Communist Manifesto.* Cambridge University Press: England.

Rutham, V.W. 1990. "Models of Agricultural Development," in Eicher, C.K. et al (1990). *Agricultural Development in the Third World. Baltimore*: John Hopkins University Press.

Sahlins, M. 1972. *Stone Age Economics*. London: Frank Cass.

Schatz, S. P. 1977. *Nigerian Capitalism*. Berkeley: UCLA Press.

Seidman, A., et al.1986. *Aid and Development*. Trenton: Africa World Press.

_____ and Anang, F. (eds.). 1992. *Towards a New Vision of Self-Sustainable Development*. Trenton, New Jersey: Africa World Press.

Shanim, T. (ed.). 1971. *Peasants and Peasant Societies*. London: Penguin Books.

Shaw, T. and Adedeji, A.(eds.) 1988. *Economic Crisis in Africa: African Perspectives in Development Problems and Potentials*. Boulder, Colorado: L. Reinner Publishers.

Shiva, Vandana. 1989. "Development: the new colonialism," in *Development, (Journal of the Society for International Development, Rome)* 1, pp. 84-87.

Snyder, M.C, and Tadesse, M. 1995. *African Women and Development*. London: Zed Press.

Stavenhagen, R. 1973. "Classes, Colonialism, and Acculturation,." in *Studies in Comparative International Development,* Vol.1, 6. pp.53-77

Suleiman, M. (ed.) 1991. *Africa Vol II: Environment and Women,* IFAA.

Szentes, T. 1971. *The Political Economy of Underdevelopment*. Budepest: Hungarian Academy of Sciences.

Tanzer, M. 1980. "Oil Exploration Strategies: Alternative Strategies for the Third World," in T. Turner and P. Nore (eds.), *Oil and Class Struggle*. London: Zed Press.

_____ 1980. *The Race for Resources*. New York: Monthly Review Press.

Bibliography

Taylor, R.T. 1988. *Hot Money and the Politics of Development*. London: Zed Press.

Trager, L. and Osinulu, C. "New women's organizations in Nigeria: one response to structural adjustment," in Christina H. Gladwin (ed.), *Structural adjustment and African women farmers*. Gainesville: University of Florida Press, 1991, pp. 339-358.

Turner, T. 1978. "Commercial Capitalism and the 1975 Coup," in K. Panther-Brick, (ed..) *Soldiers and Oil*. London: Frank Cass.

_____ 1980. "Nigeria: Imperialism, Oil Technology and the Comprador State." *Oil and Class Struggle*. London: Zed Press.

_____ and P. Nore (eds.) 1980. *Oil and Class Struggle*. London: Zed Press.

Turner, T. and Badru, P. 1985 "Oil and Instability: Class Contradictions and the 1983 Coup", in *Journal of African Marxists*, London, England. pp.4-34.

United Bank for Africa, 1990. *Monthly Business and Economic Digest*. (Various issues, 1990-1992. Lagos: Nigeria).

Wallerstein, I. 1974. *The Origin of the Modern World System: Capitalist Agriculture and the Origins of the European World- Economy in the Sixteenth Century*. New York: Academy Press.

_____ 1979. *The Capitalist World Economy*. New York: Cambridge University Press.

_____ 1984. *The Politics of the World- Economy: The States, the Movements, and the Civilizations*. Cambridge: Cambridge University Press.

_____ 1986. *The Three Stages of Africa Involvement in the World Economy*. Trenton, New Jersey: Third World Press.

Warrens, B. 1980. *Imperialism, Pioneer of Capitalism*. London: New Left Books.

Watts, M. 1987. *State,Oil and Agriculture in Nigeria*. Berkeley: University of California Press.

Wilber, C.K. 1965. "Development and Stagnation in Latin America: a Structural Approach." in *Studies in Comparative Development*, no.1, 11.

_____ 1970. *Economic Development of Latin America*. Cambridge: Cambridge Press.

_____ 1973. *The Political Economy of Development and Underdevelopment*. New York: Random House.

Williams, G. 1980. *State and Society in Nigeria*. Nigeria: Afrographical Publishers.

_____ 1980. "Inequalities in Rural Nigeria". Report prepared for the International Labor organization. Oxford: Oxford University Press.

_____ (ed.). 1976. Nigeria: *Economy and Society*. London. Rex Collings.

_____ 1987. "The World Bank in Rural Nigeria: A review of the World Bank's Nigerian Agricultural Sector." *Occasional papers*, St. Peter's College, Oxford.

_____ (Undated) "Why is there no Agrarian Capitalism in Nigeria?" *Occasional papers*, University of Ibadan, Nigeria.

_____ 1981. "The World Bank and the Peasant Problem," in *Rural Development in Africa*, eds. P. Heyer et al. New York: St. Martin Press.

Wisner, B. 1989. *Power and Need in Africa: Basic Human Needs and Development Policies*. Trenton, New Jersey: Africa World Press

Wolpe, H. 1975. "The Theory of Internal Colonialism: The South African Case," in I, Oxaal , T. Barnett, and D. Boots (eds.), *Beyond the Sociology of Development*. London and Boston: Routledge and Kegan Paul.

World Bank. 1978. *World Bank's Document No.1525-UNI*. Appraisal of

Nucleus Estate/Smallholder Oil Palm Project in Rivers State, Nigeria.

_____ 1983. *Sub-saharan Africa-Progress Report on Development: Prospects and Programmes.* Washington, D.C.

_____ 1981. *Accelerated Development in Sub-saharan Africa.*

_____ 1989. *Sub-Saharan Africa: From Crisis to Sustainable Growth.* Washington, D.C.

_____ *World Bank Special Memorandum on the Agricultural Sector in Nigeria,* Vol.I, June 15, 1984.

_____ 1990. *Making Adjustment Work for the Poor.* Washington, D.C.

_____ 1986. *World Debt Tables.* Washington, D.C.

_____ 1990. *Financing Adjustment with Growth in Sub-Saharan Africa,* 1986-1990. Washington, D.C.

_____ 1990. *Social Indicators of Development 1990.* Washington, D.C.

_____ 1990. *Annual Report: Trends in Developing Economies.* Washington, D.C.

_____ 1991. *World Development Report: The Challenge of Development.* Washington, D.C.

_____ 1991. *Annual Report.* Washington, DC.

_____ 1991. *Global Economic Prospects and the Developing Countries.* Washington, D.C.

_____ 1996. *The World Bank Participation Source Book.* Washington, D.C.

Appendix

1. Household #. Study sheet number #

2. Size of household

    1. Total household members
    2. Total number of female members
    3. Total numbers of male members

3. Sex   1. Female   2. Male

4. Age:

    12-14
    15-19
    20-29
    30-39
    40-49
    50-59
    60-69
    70+

5. Marital Status: 1. Single   2. Married

6. How many Wives? _____

7. Religion

   1. Christian
   2. Muslim
   3. Traditional
   4. Others- (specify)
   5. None

8. Education

   School years completed overall by female

   1. Primary school (six years completed)
   2. Primary school (less than six years completed)
   3. Secondary modern school completed
   4. Less than secondary modern school completed
   5. Government awarded G.4 certificate
   6. West African School certificate
   7. Some college
   8. College degree

9. School years completed overall by male

   1. Primary school (six years completed)
   2. Primary school (less than six years completed)
   3. Secondary modern school completed
   4. Less than secondary modern school completed
   5. Government awarded G.4 certificate
   6. West African School certificate
   7. Some college
   8. College degree
   9. Advanced college degree
   10. Teachers' certification degree
   11. No education

10. Occupation

    1. Upland farming
    2. Fadama farming
    3. Livestock farming
    4. Fish farming
    5. Trading
    6. Artisan
    7. Civil Servant
    8. Others (specify)

11. Living conditions

    Housing ownership

        1. Owned   2. Inherited   3. Rented
        4. Others.........

    Type of housing

        1. Mud, thatched roof
        2. Mud, zinz roof
        3. Cement block/bricks/zinc roof
        4. Others (specify)...

12. Means of transportation:

        1. Bicycle
        2. Motorcycle
        3. Car
        4. Lorry
        5. Pick up
        6. Animal
        7. Public transportation

13. Labour force per household (able bodied)
    1. Total labour force in agriculture
    2. Female members engaged in agriculture
    3. Male members engaged in agriculture
    4. Number of household members working outside of the family farm

14. Household income

    1. Total household income
    2. Share top 10 percent by gender
    3. Share top 20 percent by gender
    4. Share bottom 40 percent by gender
    5. Share bottom 20 percent by gender

15. Sources of household income

    1. Farm produce
    2. Fishing and seasonal employment
    3. Wage employment at the main estate
    4. Government employment
    5. Trading traditional (female)
    6. City Trading (male)

16. Occupational categories

    1. Bricklayers and dressmakers
    2. Barber
    3. Motor vehicle driver
    4. Owner/motor vehicle driver
    5. Merchant
    6. Painter
    7. Mechanic and mechanic assistants
    8. Law enforcement
    9. Street vendors
    10. Civil service and other white collar

17. Household level of protein consumption

    1. Traditional staples- calories per household
    2. Meat, fish, milk, eggs etc.
    3. Cereal consumption (wheat, barley, yellow corn)
    4. Imported food items

18. Access to medical facilities

    1. Distance from the local clinic
    2. Distance from municipal health centre
    3. Distance from the general hospital
    4. Distance from the teaching hospital

19. Rural Infrastructure and transportation

    1. Distance from feeder roads
    2. Distance from railroad
    3. Owned car
    4. Owned motorcycle
    5. Owned bicycle
    6. Relied on public transportation

20. Access to portable drinking water

    1. Household fitted with pipe bore water
    2. Household own borehole (well)
    3. Share borehole with other families
    4. Household relies on community borehole
    5. Household travels more than five kilometres to the nearest clean water
    6. House relies on village nearby stream
    7. Household relies on untreated water from nearby ponds

21. Electricity

    1. Household connected to government electrification system

    2. Household linked to electricity at the main estate

    3. Household owns power generator

    4. Household has no source of modern electricity

22. Accessibility to farm equipment

    1. Household either owns or has the use of one or more of these agricultural equipments

    Tractor
    Combined harvester
    Electric mower
    Water or irrigation pump
    Hoses and cutlasses
    None of the above

23. Services from the extension workers

    1. 0-1 visit a week

    2. 2-5 visits a week

    3. more than five days in a week

24. Peasant farmers' perception of the advice they receive from the extension workers

    1. very good

    2. good

    3. moderately good

    4. not good

    5. very bad

25. Household use of other peasants' labour

    1. employ only household members

    2. employ relatives who are paid for their services

    3. household relies partly on family labour and seasonal wage labourers

4. household uses only wage labourers

26. Sources of improved seeds last season

    1. Own production from previous year's crop
    2. Bought from the ADP
    3. Bought from MANR
    4. Bought from market/dealer
    5. Others (specify) ....

27. Sources of fertilizer and other inputs

    1. Bought from the ADP
    2. Bought from MANR
    3. Bought from market/dealer
    4. Others (specify) ....

28. Sources of credit last season

    1. ADP
    2. MANR
    3. ACB
    4. People's Bank
    5. Friends/relative
    6. Money Lenders
    7. Community Bank
    8. Other Commercial Banks
    9. None needed
    10. None was available ....

29. Farm detail

    1. Total number of fields owned ....
    (both cultivated and uncultivated)
    2. Number of fields cultivated ....
    3. Total area under cultivation (in hectares)
    4. List below the important crops grown and area (ha) in the fields

Area (ha) (i)   ....
       (ii)   ....
      (iii)   ....
      (iv)   ....

30. Quantity farm produce (Tonne) the previous year

      (i)   ....
      (ii)   ....
     (iii)   ....
      (iv)   ....
      (v)   ....

31. Extension contact

    1. Do you know the Extension Agent in your area?
       1.Yes   2. No

    2.   If yes, how long have you known him?
       1. this year
       2. last year
       3. three years ago
       4. more than three years ago

32.   Do you know any contact farmer in your ward or village?

    1.Yes   2. No

33. If you answer yes to question 29 above, have you ever discussed with the contact farmer on messages received from Extension Agents?

    1.Yes   2. No

34. Sources of information on new technology.

For each of the following answer "yes" if you receive/have ever received information on new farm technology and "no" if you have not.

1. Contact Farmer
   1.Yes   2. No

2. Extension Agent
   1.Yes   2. No

3. Relatives
   1.Yes   2. No

4. Friends
   1.Yes   2. No

5. Extension publication
   1.Yes   2. No

6. SPATS/demonstration plots
   1. Yes 2. No

7. Field days/Extension group meeting
   1.Yes   2. No

8. Agric Shows
   1.Yes   2. No

9. Sales agent
   1.Yes   2. No

10. Television
    1. Yes 2. No

11. Radio
    1. Yes   2. No

12. Local Market/festivals
    1.Yes   2. No

35. Knowledge about improved technology. Answer "yes" if you have any knowledge about the following or "no" if you have not.

   1. Improved farm practices
    1. Yes   2. No

   2. Improved Crop variety
    1.Yes   2. No

   3. Seed dressing
    1.Yes   2. No

   4. Fertilizer application
    1.Yes   2. No

   5. Use of other agrochemicals
    1.Yes   2. No

   6. Processing and Storage techniques
    1.Yes   2. No

   7. Harvesting techniques
    1.Yes   2. No

   8. Livestock production
    1.Yes   2. No

   9. Fish production
    1.Yes   2. No

Index

153

For Product Safety Concerns and Information please contact our EU
representative GPSR@taylorandfrancis.com Taylor & Francis Verlag GmbH,
Kaufingerstraße 24, 80331 München, Germany

Printed and bound by CPI Group (UK) Ltd, Croydon, CR0 4YY

13/05/2025

01869648-0001